Golf
in the zone
Get your game and your mind
in the right place to win

A DAVID & CHARLES BOOK
Copyright © David & Charles Limited 2007

David & Charles is an F+W Publications Inc. company
4700 East Galbraith Road
Cincinnati, OH 45236

First published in 2007

Source material courtesy of *Today's Golfer* magazine © Emap Active
Photography by Bob Atkins

A catalogue record for this book is available from the British Library.

ISBN-13: 978-0-7153-2541-4
ISBN-10: 0-7153-2541-8

Printed in China by Shenzhen Donnelley Printing Co Ltd
for David & Charles
Brunel House   Newton Abbot   Devon

Commissioning Editor: Neil Baber
Art Editor: Marieclare Mayne
Assistant Editor: Louise Clark
Copy Editor: Nick Fawcett
Production Controller: Kelly Smith

Visit our website at www.davidandcharles.co.uk

David & Charles books are available from all good bookshops; alternatively you can
contact our Orderline on 0870 9908222 or write to us at FREEPOST EX2 110,
D&C Direct, Newton Abbot, TQ12 4ZZ (no stamp required UK only); US customers
call 800-289-0963 and Canadian customers call 800-840-5220.

Golf
in the zone
Get your game and your mind in the right place to win

Adrian Fryer & Dr Karl Morris

D&C
David and Charles

GAMEZONE

MINDZONE

BIOGRAPHIES

CONTENTS

Introduction

Golf looks such a simple game, or at least it does when you watch the experts at work. Whether it's Tiger Woods launching a drive off the tee, Ernie Els splashing out of a bunker, Phil Mickelson playing an exquisite lob or Colin Montgomerie landing yet another iron shot close to the pin, it all seems effortless. Try such shots ourselves though, and we soon learn otherwise.

Let's face it; we could all improve our golf. Few of us are all-rounders, and most of us spend our lives searching for those magic moves to make the game easier. So what's the secret of playing like a champion? Some say it's down to technique, others that it's all in the mind. The truth is that both are right and both are wrong. Sound technique is vital if we're to play good golf, but so also is a cool head, being able to cope with pressure and harness the power of the psyche. The two are inextricably linked.

There's no use spending hours on the range perfecting your technique if you can't control your nerves with a scorecard in hand. That's why we've teamed up with top sports psychologist Karl Morris and respected teaching professional Adrian Fryer to bring you the most comprehensive guide to both the mental and physical demands of playing better golf.

Game Zone, written by Adrian Fryer, hones in on technical problems, offering instruction on issues close to every golfer's heart: how to swing properly, overcome that dreaded slice, hit the ball further, play from a greenside bunker, chip more reliably, and so forth. Mind Zone, written by Dr Karl Morris, tackles the mental side of golf – an area too often overlooked. As well as outlining visualization techniques that can help improve our performance even when we're miles from a golf course, it explores in depth the massive impact temperament and attitude can have on our game. A host of invaluable tips, employed by many of the world's leading players, show how we channel these to work *for* rather than *against* us.

Use this book to learn new shots and skills, to iron out those bad habits that have been niggling you for years and simply to make your golf more enjoyable. Get your game straight and your mind in the right place and better scores will surely follow. And once you are playing 'golf in the zone', perhaps it will feel like a simple game after all.

Carly Cummins
Instruction Editor *Today's Golfer*

GAMEZONE

Set-up, alignment, backswing, followthrough – for most golfers these are a minefield, the harder they work at their technique the more confused they become. If that's your experience don't despair, for in the following pages celebrated instructor Adrian Fryer offers expert guidance that will unlock the mysteries of this wonderful sport, making the complicated suddenly seem easy. Like countless top-class professionals, you will find here advice to transform your game.

Keep it simple to swing on track

Most amateurs hit across the ball, often on an out-to-in swing track that brings on a slice. In fact, any across-the-line swing means loss of distance and unwanted sidespin. Even if you are careful to stand square to your target line at address, it is still possible to swing the club off-line. Almost always, golfers send their swing off-line by making it more complicated than it needs to be. I am going to show you how to simplify not only your swing but also your understanding of that horror phrase 'swing plane'. You will learn how to cut out much unneeded movement, and so to swing consistently on track.

AS USED BY... **DAVID TOMS**

Next time you watch this elegant American play, take a look at his left arm
halfway back. You'll see a great position and a perfect swing plane.

Left arm checkpoint

CHECK 1: A great way to check if your swing begins on-line is to focus on your left arm. Place a club by your feet to represent your target line, and set up to a ball. Now make a half-backswing, your left arm parallel to the ground. When your backswing is on-line your left arm should be just a little inside parallel to the shaft on the ground.

CHECK 2: If your left arm sticks out across the shaft on the ground, you will almost certainly have the club in a flat position, its shaft more horizontal than at address. This often happens because you are striving too hard for width.

CHECK 3: If your left arm line is way inside the clubshaft you will put the club in an upright position, shaft more vertical than at address. You may be trying too hard to get the club inside the line on the backswing.

SWING PLANE

Grab your 6 & 7-iron

Hold the 6-iron in your left hand and set up to a ball with the sole flat on the ground. The angle of the shaft represents the ideal angle for the club to swing on; this is your 'swing plane'. Hold the 7-iron with your right hand. Make a half-backswing, till your hand is at chest height. Aim to get the 7-iron shaft mimicking the angle of the 6. This represents an on-line backswing. If necessary, ask a friend to help you find this position.

Common error 1: too flat

Many golfers have a notion they must get on the 'inside' during the backswing. This thought usually leads to your wrists rolling the club into a very flat position during the backswing, the clubshaft more horizontal than at set-up. Set the club on this path and you'll need some serious adjustments to get the club back to the ball on a good line. This is more an 'inswing' than a backswing. It will mean loss of distance and a load of unwanted sidespin.

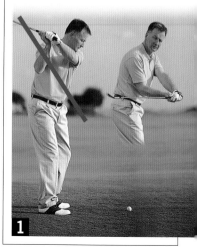

1

2

Common error 2: too upright

Other golfers have been told to swing the clubhead straight back in an effort to keep the club on-line for as long as possible. But this puts the shaft in an upright position halfway back, more vertical than at address. Again, you'll need to build in some in-swing compensations as you return to the ball, which leads to inconsistency. You could call this an 'out-swing'. Again, as with any across-the-line swing, it will reduce distance and increase the risk of a slice.

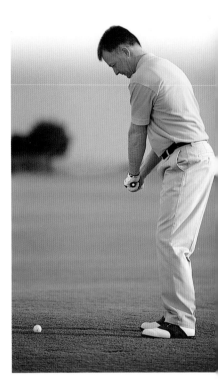

Don't complicate it!

As you see, these errors crop up when you try to follow supposed 'advice'. If you weren't trying to do anything with your backswing, you'd probably swing it back pretty well. Remember, it is called a backswing because you swing the club back as your body turns. Keep this simple thought in your head.

HEAD FOLLOWS BUTT

Quick tip

Your ability to learn new positions is much improved when you can picture them clearly in your head. Studying these pictures of Adrian will help you find good positions when you practise.

A key downswing thought is that the clubhead follows the butt of the club as it swings down. If you swing the club back on the correct shaft angle you will swing through this position.

From here you can see how easy it is to swing down into the ball on the correct path, the clubhead following my hands. The clubshaft is mirroring the angle it was on at address.

WHAT'S YOUR PROBLEM?

You can't see your top-of-the-backswing position or your downswing, so if you are inconsistent it can be hard to know where your problem lies. Try this guide.

1) If halfway down your body feels in the way of your swing; your hands and arms feel very close to your right side; a tee peg stuck into the butt of the club points down at your shoes instead of behind the ball; the clubshaft is very vertical…

2: If halfway down the club feels miles away from you; the right elbow is floating away from your right hip; you feel very 'outside the line', as though you will hit the ball left; the tee peg in the butt of your club points forwards rather than at the ground…

1a)…then at the top you would have been across-the-line (clubshaft pointing right of target).

2a)…then at the top you would have been in this position, known as laid-off (club pointing way left of the target).

Underdo, overdo it for a good swing

One of the most common questions I am asked is, 'How can I feel if I am in a good position?' Unfortunately, in the golf swing, positions that feel great can often be wrong and sometimes a correct position can feel strange because it is new. The best method to feel the correct position is for you to underdo a movement, then overdo it, and finally, strike a happy medium between the two.

HEAD MOVEMENT

Your head is heavy and can dictate the form and balance of your swing. Yet many golfers do not know how much their head should move in the swing, and even more are unaware of how much their head actually is moving.

Keep your head still

Take your driver and aim to make a backswing without moving your head at all. You will find it tough, and restrictive. It is almost impossible to make a full turn without moving your head slightly.

Move your head across

This time allow your head to move to your right, so that your left ear is pretty much where your right ear was at address – in other words, a full head's-width away. You'll feel unrestricted but a little loose and sloppy.

Split the difference

Ideally your head will move about half a head's-width to the right, your left ear replacing where your nose was at address. This will give you freedom to move and turn, but enough stability to coil into your right side without swaying. You will find it much easier to achieve this once you have felt the first two positions.

Quick tip

Underdoing and overdoing a move is a great way to learn because the feelings send your brain reference points. It can then easily work out a successful middle ground.

3

LEFT-HAND GRIP

Your grip controls the clubface, which controls the ball. A poor grip can lead to off-line hits. Grab a tee peg and stick it between your thumb and index finger. This is going to be your guide.

Tee at 12 o'clock

Imagine a clockface running around your left hand, your wrist in the centre. When the peg points straight down the shaft (as you look from above) to 12 o'clock, this represents what is known as a 'weak' grip. It's called weak because it will tend to deliver the clubface in an open position, aiming right of your target, adding loft to the face. Shots go high, right and short.

Tee at 2 o'clock

Your left hand is now in a 'strong' position, so-called because this grip will usually return the club to the ball in a closed position, aiming left of the target and with reduced clubface loft. The ball will tend to come out low and hooking and with more distance than a square face would produce.

Quick tip

Learning anything new is never easy, especially when we've got into the habit of doing it in a certain way. Underdoing and then overdoing it can be invaluable in striking a happy medium.

3

Split the difference: Tee at 1 o'clock

Make sure your grip is somewhere between those two extremes. Again, do not think in terms of rights and wrongs. But why not start out by trying to make that tee peg point exactly between the first two positions, pointing to around 1 o'clock. This will give you your best chance of returning the clubface square to the ball every time.

The top of the backswing is a great position to check whether or not your swing is on track. An over-upright or flat backswing means you have to make in-swing compensations to swing through on a good path.

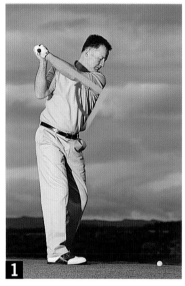

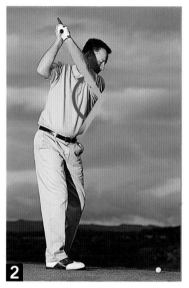

Swing flat

Make an exaggerated flat backswing. Imagine that at the top, your left forearm will be no higher than your right shoulder, perhaps even a little below it. It's not impossible to hit a decent shot from this position, but this is as flat as you want to go. Try this backswing five times.

Swing upright

Now do the opposite. Swing up steeply, as if you were trying to swing your left forearm towards your right ear. Again, there are ways of rescuing the shot from this position – the American Jim Furyk manages it brilliantly – but unless you've got all day to practise, you're going to be inconsistent.

Split the difference

By now you will know what an upright and a flat backswing both feel like, and you will have in your mind's eye a slot or channel between the two for the club to travel in. Go ahead and make five backswings, hitting that slot every time. Don't feel you have to find one perfect position; anywhere in that channel will represent an on-line backswing.

3

How can you tell if you are swinging straight through to your target? Again, the best way is to hit left, hit right and then split the difference. Set up two balls in a line to your target, three feet apart, then place two more a foot either side of the ball nearest the target.

Left gate

Imagine the middle ball and the left-hand ball are forming a gate. Hit five shots, trying to smack the ball through the gate every time. This will bring home to you the feeling of hitting the ball left of the target.

Right gate

Now do the same thing on the other side. Hit balls through the right-hand 'goal'. Keep going until you have scored with five balls in a row.

AS USED BY... **TONY JOHNSTONE**

The Zimbabwean uses a version of this drill when he lines up his body at address. Watch him closely and you will see he begins by taking his stance with feet and body miles shut (aiming right of the target). He then swivels round until he aims miles open (left of the target), before splitting the difference and aiming straight down the fairway. It's worth a try if you have regular trouble aiming your feet, hips and shoulders.

3

Split the difference: Middle gate

You have trained your muscles to recognize a swing to the left and a swing to the right. Now let them find a happy medium as you aim to hit over the middle ball. Even if the ball doesn't fly dead straight, you have given yourself a much better concept of a down-the-line throughswing.

Use your elbows as reference points

You can improve your swing dramatically by focusing on your elbows. They act as superb reference points throughout the swing. Not only are you able to spot many of the golf swing's major flaws through monitoring your elbow positions, you can also improve your action by training your elbows to work in certain ways and through certain positions. Once you know what to look for you can use your elbows to square up your alignment, improve your swing plane, control your swing length and swell your power. And, as I will show you, it could not be simpler.

CHECKPOINT

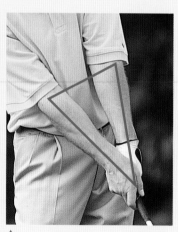

▲
Look at how far apart your elbows are and the triangle they form with your hands. Aim to keep this gap constant throughout the swing.

▲
As you swing through the ball, feel your elbows are as far apart as they were at address. The triangle between arms and shoulders should be pretty much intact.

1: ELBOW

Many golfers doom their swing before it starts by misaligning their elbows at set-up. Here's how you can make sure they start off in the correct position.

STEP 1: Take a medium iron and grip it normally. Keep your arms relaxed. Draw your elbows in to your body so that they are resting lightly on your sides just above your hips.

STEP 2: From here, simply push the clubhead gently away from you until your elbows are drawn towards each other and your arms are lightly extended. This is the perfect starting position for your elbows.

Your elbows can help you set up to the ball squarely.

Tucking the elbow in

Amateurs are often told to tuck their right elbow into their side. Usually this is done because they want to ensure they swing the club back on an inside track and avoid a slice. But this happens naturally because you are stood to the side of the ball. Try to make it happen and you will overdo it. You will swing the club back too much on the inside. It normally leads to a big loop and an out-to-in, slicing swing path.

If I was to place a clubshaft against your elbows at address I would want to see the shaft pointing parallel to your target line.

To hit the ball further, pay attention to your right elbow position at impact.

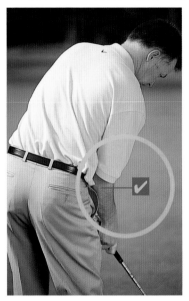

Impact

Feel your right elbow in contact with your right hip as you swing into the ball. This is a powerful position, which allows you to hold on to your stored power until impact. Think of it like a boxer throwing a punch – his elbow is tucked in to his side until the moment he lands the hit in a sudden explosion of strength.

Avoid a gap

If you feel your right elbow is away from your side as you swing in to the ball, this is a sure sign you have tried to hit the ball too early and too hard in your downswing. When you hit the ball too early and hard, your right side takes on too dominant a role, which lifts your right elbow out, inevitably resulting in loss of power.

4: ELBOW PLANE

Your right elbow can help you swing the club around your body on the correct swing plane, acting once again as a vital reference point.

STEP 1: Set up to the ball and imagine a line running from the ball past your right elbow and extending skyward. This angle represents a good swing plane. This is a good angle for you to visualize when you swing the club.

STEP 2: As you swing the club back, imagine your right elbow simply moving up and down that line as if it was on runners. You do not need to get this spot on, but stick close to this imagined line and you will go a long way to avoid swinging flat or upright.

CHECKPOINT

▶ It's a common mistake to keep your right arm straight on the takeaway in a misguided quest for width in the backswing. This locks the right elbow and leads to a stilted, over-upright takeaway.

▼ Ensure your elbow bone looks at your hip bone at set-up. When you take the club away, allow the joint to fold so the elbow points down at the ground to allow you to coil fully, powerfully and on plane.

Quick tip

If you have trouble visualizing this elbow action, imagine how your elbow moves when you use a hammer: simply up and down in a line and not from side to side.

Overswinging is a huge factor in poorly executed shots. Once again, paying attention to your right elbow can help you overcome this.

Keep it in sight

Swing to the top and check your elbows. You should be able to see your right elbow comfortably, folded to pretty much a right angle and pointing to the ground. This shows your backswing is not too long.

Check at the top

If your elbow is out of sight, this is a clear sign you have swung back too far. Once your right elbow moves round behind you it will take the left arm with it, causing you to lose control.

Quick tip

Imagine yourself throwing a tennis ball. As you take your arm back your elbow points back behind you. Aim to build this feeling into your golf swing. The results will speak for themselves.

Turn and see

Here is another way of checking. Place a golf club under your right bicep, shaft sticking out on the same line. Make your normal backswing turn. Your right elbow should point away from the target and a little behind you.

Check behind

If you make your backswing turn and discover that the shaft is pointing right round behind you, shaft at right angles to your target, you have gone too far. Practise keeping your right elbow in front of your turning body.

Learn from your finish

The golf swing is a chain reaction. It follows that faults during your action show up at the end, while good swing moves also reveal themselves through a full yet balanced finish. By analysing your followthrough position you can learn a whole lot about your swing. Of course we golfers finish our swings in all kinds of different positions, but I believe amateurs fall into four major categories. I describe them here, and explain which swing flaws will lead you to that end. Decide which position looks most familiar to you and work through my simple drills to rid yourself of the problem. You will find working backwards can be your best route forwards.

WHAT YOU'RE AFTER ...
THE PERFECT FINISH

CLUB SHAFT – pretty much on the same angle as your eyes

HANDS – over left shoulder, revealing the club has been swung on a good plane round the body

BELT BUCKLE – pointing at target or slightly left of it, showing controlled body rotation through the ball

ELBOWS – the same distance apart they were at address, revealing arms and body have stayed 'connected' through the swing

WEIGHT – balanced on the outside of your front heel, revealing good weight movement in harmony with the motion of the club

RIGHT FOOT – vertical, toe on the ground, revealing the correct amount of body rotation through the shot

LOWER-BODY SLIDER

You are delivering the club too much from an inside path. When your hands and arms swing down towards the ball they are almost behind your right side, and your right elbow gets stuck behind your right hip. You will feel in your own way and have no option but to slide your lower body forwards in order to create the room for your arms to swing down and through.

How to cure it...

You must turn through the shot better. Think of it as looking for a more rotational movement through impact rather than a sliding one where your left side moves towards the hole. Try this drill.

STEP 1: Stick an umbrella into the ground next to the outside of your left (front) foot.

STEP 2: Rehearse a downswing where your left hip rotates behind you and out of your way. It can move towards the brolly before turning inside it. Your old, sliding action would send your left hip straight into the brolly. Practise this downswing until you can keep your left hip turning away to your left and not butting the umbrella.

UPRIGHT FINISH – hands very high, almost above your left ear

WEIGHT – very much on the outside of your front foot

ARCHED BACK – your spine will form a reverse C as your lower body slides forward

LEG COLLAPSE – knees will be over-bent and restrict a powerful unwinding of the hips

RIGHT FOOT – slides towards the target as your legs slide

WHAT SHOTS DOES IT CAUSE?

You will hit hooks and pushes (shots that head straight right). It can also lead to fat and thin shots. You will have difficulty taking a divot. If you do manage one it may point right of your target.

This is usually the result when a golfer practically hurls himself at the ball to try and clout it into next week. His over-dominant right shoulder whirls round into the ball and carries on afterwards, causing the entire right side to follow over the top.

How to cure it...

You must train your right elbow and shoulder to work down and under your chin, rather than around and in front of it. Here is a simple throwing drill to teach you the correct sensations.

STEP 1: Hold a golf ball in your right hand. Without a club, set up to a ball with your normal address position. Make your swing. Your goal is to throw the ball in your right hand so that it hits the ball on the ground.

STEP 2: It will feel to you like you are trying to bounce the ball out to the right of your target line. When you get it right you'll feel your right shoulder in a position where it can work down and under your chin as you release the ball. Your old out-and-around, right shoulder-dominated throughswing will make you throw the ball well to the left of the ball on the ground. Work on this drill until you are consistently throwing the ball out to the right of your target line.

SHOULDERS – much further towards the hole than your hips

RIGHT SHOULDER – high and dominant, knocking your head up and out of the way

BACK – straightened up so spine is vertical

WEIGHT – too much on your front foot, perhaps even toppling forward

RIGHT LEG – straightens as the body leans forward

RIGHT SHOE – flopped out as the upper body takes over

WHAT SHOTS DOES IT CAUSE?

You'll find yourself hitting pulls (straight left), cuts and slices and taking deep divots which may point left of your target line.

BACK-FOOT SCOOPER

This position is almost always found by a golfer trying to lift the ball into the air. His weight stays back, behind the ball, while he flicks the clubhead forward past his hands and wrists in a misguided effort to lift the ball skyward. Remember, the loft on the clubface gets the ball airborne for you.

How to cure it...

First you must learn to trust the loft of the clubface to do the job for you. But also you need to change your angle of attack into the ball so that your iron clubhead is actually swinging down towards the turf as it strikes the ball. A tee peg can help you.

STEP 1: Push a tee peg into the ground on your ball-to-target line and opposite the outside of your left foot.

STEP 2: Make your normal swing and hit the ball, but make your main mission to knock the tee peg out of the ground as the club swings past impact. Chances are your clubhead will swing over the top the first few times, but as you practise this you will feel your weight moving forward properly as you swing through to help the clubhead meet the tee. Your old scooping action would send the clubhead up over the tee peg every time. If you are struggling, try the drill without the ball. Just focus on knocking that tee peg out of the ground.

Quick tip

Make it your policy to watch and really enjoy a good shot. Emotion enhances your memory, so the more you enjoy a good shot the better your chances of remembering and repeating it.

ELBOWS – very close in to the body

STOMACH – facing right of the target

WEIGHT – stays on the back foot

WHAT SHOTS DOES IT CAUSE?

You will hit plenty of high-flying, weak shots. You will also be prone to striking turf before ball and thinning the shot, because your scooping action means the club has reached the bottom of its arc and is climbing by the time it meets the ball.

BACK-FOOT SLICER

This golfer tries to keep the clubface looking at the target through the ball. As he follows through, the badge of the glove faces the sky with the right hand underneath the grip. This leads to what's known as the 'chicken wing' – the left elbow sticks up and away from the side of the body. The clubface is therefore open at impact, the ball slices from left to right and, in an attempt to compensate, the golfer hangs back on his back foot to start the ball left.

How to cure it...

STEP 1: Rotate your forearms through impact. Rehearse this position, where your right hand rolls over the top of your left. Note how your left elbow folds into your left side. This shows good rotation of the forearm and will help you to get that clubface squared up at impact for straighter shots.

STEP 2: Work your right heel forward. Stick a tee peg just outside your back heel. Practise making a throughswing where your right heel works forward, away from the tee. This promotes the correct rolling foot action as weight rotates into your front foot. If you find your right heel swings back and knocks the tee peg over as you follow through, this reveals to you that your weight is hanging back too much in your swing. Try practising without the ball, moving your weight correctly and feeling how good footwork improves your balance and power.

ELBOWS – splayed, as your stunted followthrough forces them apart

WEIGHT – stuck on your back foot

HIPS – facing right of the target, showing short followthrough

WHAT SHOTS DOES IT CAUSE?

You will hit pulls with your short irons and big slices with the long stuff. Your divots will aim left.

Quick tip

Your finishing position is a barometer of the tension in your swing. Check your hands and arms. If your muscles are tight, it reveals you have been squeezing the club too hard during the swing.

Kill your slice

Your ball slices for one reason only; your clubface is open (facing to the right for right-handers) to the path it is swinging on. An open clubface gives the ball only a weak, glancing blow that sends it spinning off right towards the trees. Trying to keep the clubface facing your target through the ball can directly cause this open face. In fact the face constantly rotates through the swing, and if you are to cure your slice you must develop the feeling of the clubface rotating from an open to a shut (aiming left of the target for right-handers) position through impact. Once you gain confidence from seeing the ball spin to the left instead of the right, you can work on the path of your swing to allow for the right-to-left spin you are generating. Follow this plan and you really will find that elusive draw shape.

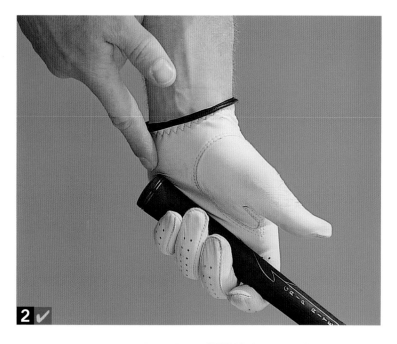

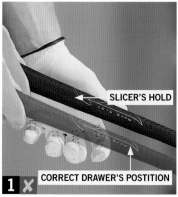

SLICER'S HOLD

CORRECT DRAWER'S POSTITION

CHECK 1: Check your left-hand grip. In the classic slicer's position it runs high up in the hand, through the palm or even along the left thumb pad. This very weak hold stops your wrists hinging correctly and leads to that dreaded open clubface position at impact.

CHECK 2: Make sure you hold the club in the fingers of your left hand, not the palm, and that the heel of your hand – that fleshy bit bottom right – folds over on top of the grip. This is what guarantees your ability to use your wrists as a powerful lever. NEVER let the heel slip down by the side of the grip.

Ensure that the leading edge of the clubface is vertical.

Note how the clubface rotates shut as your left wrist straightens.

Left hand only

Grip the club with left hand only and hold it out in front of you so that the clubface's leading edge is vertical. Look down at your left hand. Do you notice a little kink in your left wrist? This comes from placing the heel of your left hand on top of the grip. It may seem small but this kink plays a crucial role.

Shutting the toe

Push the club away from you so that your arm and the shaft become almost straight and your left wrist flattens. This mimics what happens in your swing as you move through impact. See what happens to the clubface? It closes. The toe turns over into a slightly 'shut' position, perfect for a right-to-left drawspin.

AS USED BY... JOHN DALY

The big-hitting American achieves his draw shape with just this move – a rotation of the left arm while the left wrist flattens and the clubface turns over.

Check the toe has overtaken the heel shortly after impact.

STEP 1: I want you to work on this feeling of pushing out down the shaft and feeling the clubface rotating from open to closed through impact. Without a ball, take a lofted iron. Grip it with that wrist kink. Make a short backswing, hands no higher than hip height.

STEP 2: Make a slow-motion move through the impact zone. Feel you are pushing the club away from you, your left arm extending and rotating. Sense your left wrist flattening and the clubface closing. Remember, the face rotates all the time, reaching a square position for only the briefest of moments at impact.

STEP 3: Now try hitting some 20–30 yard shots. Aim to put a little right-to-left spin on the ball as you rotate the face.

Try it at home

Remind yourself of this rotation feeling as much as possible. Try it in front of a mirror at home, always checking that the toe of the clubface starts to turn over as your left arm stretches and rotates.

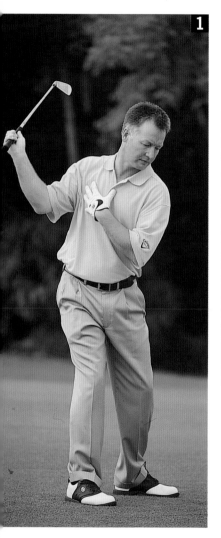

STEP 1: Develop the feeling of turning your right shoulder behind your neck. This will move your arms behind you at the top, keeping your swing on an inside, drawing swing path. If your shoulders don't turn, you bring on a steep, slicing angle of attack.

STEP 2: Try this left-hand-only backswing. At set-up place the index finger of your right hand on your left shoulder, pointing towards the target. Make your backswing. Keep turning until your index finger points behind and above the ball.

Quick tip

Fear of slicing can tighten your muscles, which shortens your backswing and actually brings it on. Take three deep breaths from the stomach before you swing to calm yourself down.

A full shoulder turn keeps your swing on track and helps you attack the ball from an inside path.

Get in sync

Most slicers have their downswings out of sync. Their upper body moves way too fast while the hands and arms lag behind. This leads to that familiar and horrible 'over-the-top' feeling, your right shoulder moving aggressively through the ball way before your arms and hands. It makes you swing across the ball to the left, the classic slicer's swing path. Here's a cure to even it up.

Quick tip

Get your downswing out of sync and you're heading for a slice. To correct this, hold back your body until your hands and arms have swung through.

This is the classic slicer's position, upper body racing ahead of arms on the way down.

Success! Right-to-left spin generates that elusive draw shape.

STEP 1: Stick an umbrella in the ground in front of your left little toe. Without a ball, take a 7-iron and make a half-backswing.

STEP 2: As you follow through, do not allow any part of your hands or body to touch the brolly. You will find your hands and arms speed the club up while your body must slow down to avoid touching the umbrella. As you start to get the hang of it, take the brolly away. But be warned – your tendency will still be to lunge with your shoulders, so swing less aggressively for a while.

SWING PATH

TARGET LINE

Swing from 'inside'

Many slicers confuse the target line with their swing path. The target line is an imaginary path from ball to target, but any attempt to swing down this leads to an out-to-in swing path and a slice. You are standing to the side of the ball, so must deliver the club to the ball from 'inside' (your side) of the target line. Here's a drill to make this clear.

STEP 1: Set up two clubs on the ground. Aim the shaft of the first to the target; this represents your target line. Now place the toe of the second against the shaft of the first so its leading edge is at right angles to it. This represents your swing path.

1

SWING PATH

TARGET LINE

STEP 2: Rehearse a downswing where the shaft of your club mirrors the angle of the swing-path clubshaft on the ground. Train the feeling of this position into your muscles. This will help you find it during a full-paced swing, which will mean you deliver the club correctly and powerfully from the inside, giving a much better swing path.

STEP 3: Note that the rotational movement of the golf swing will take your club back inside your target line on the followthrough, even when you feel you are swinging forward down your target line.

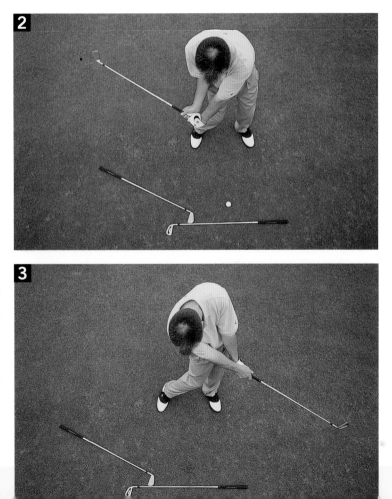

Six steps to raw power

You can start adding power to your drives before you even put the club behind the ball – and you can keep adding the oomph after the ball has been struck. You may think of power as something you need a split second before impact, but I'll show you that the process begins much earlier and ends a lot later. You'll notice that none of the six steps here asks you to hit the ball harder – but they'll all help you hit it better. Work on them and you will see your drives sailing further than ever – and with no loss of accuracy.

1: LOWER YOUR RIGHT SIDE

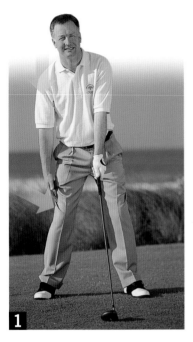

STEP 1: Kick your right knee in slightly. You will feel your right shoulder drop. This instantly places a little more weight on your back foot. Your backswing must move your weight behind the ball for maximum power, and this knee kink gives you a head start.

STEP 2: The knee kink also tilts your spine so you are leaning a little away from your target. This promotes a sweeping shot where the club is rising slightly through impact – perfect for the low-lofted driver.

STEP 3: Tee the ball up high to take advantage of this sweeping impact. Make sure at least half the ball is above the top edge of your driver.

A clean sweep

Sweep the clubhead back low to the ground for the first couple of feet as you move it away from the ball. Any 'picking up' of the clubhead with your hands and wrists can cause your hands and arms to move out of sync with your body. That means a weak, off-line swing. Remember that you are not looking to hit the ball any harder. Rhythm and timing are the key, and this smooth, sweeping action will promote just that, leading to a sweet contact and extra distance.

Left knee steady

See how little my left knee moves as I take the club away? Too much left knee movement can cause a flat, 'inside' takeaway. It will also cost you a tight, powerful coil, so make sure you resist your left knee moving in towards your right.

Quick tip

Tense hands can cause a hurried, snappy takeaway. Beat this by gripping the club as hard as you can. Your hands must relax after doing this, giving you the softness you need to sweep the club away.

Hold back the hips, turn those shoulders.

The key to a powerful coil

Take a look at the two pictures below. Clearly the picture on the right shows a much more powerful backswing than the one on the left. Coiling powerfully means increasing the differential between your hip and shoulder turns. It's all very well turning your shoulders 90°, but that's totally powerless if your hips are also turning 90°.

Here are four ways to build a more powerful coil:

1 Aim to keep your lower body as quiet as possible while turning your shoulders as far as they'll go.

2 Continue to resist the turning movement with your left knee through the backswing. This will help restrict your hip turn.

3 Your flexibility will limit your ability to make this differential. Work within your limits. You're looking for coil, not pain!

4 Hold firm with your right knee. You should feel pressure build up in your right thigh muscle – pure, powerful coiling pressure that you can release with a vengeance on the way down.

4: STAY WIDE THROUGH THE BALL

The challenge...

All powerful players hit the ball with sheer conviction, extending club and right arm down the target line just after impact. Develop this move and you will add yards to your drives. Here's a drill to help.

...the execution

Tee a ball up 18 inches in front of your normal driver position, which should be opposite your front instep. Ensure it is on your target line. Make your normal swing, but still try to meet the ball sweetly.

Measuring up

A wide swing will hit the ball further than a narrow, cramped one. The place to achieve and measure your width is at the top. Imagine there's an elastic band between the butt of your driver and your left ankle. Try to stretch this as much as possible.

Launch into the shot

Another way to build width is to try to get the butt of the club as far as possible from the target at the top. Think of it like you are throwing a javelin, really stretching back before launching forwards.

Rotate and release

Powerful hitters gain clubhead speed by rotating their hips powerfully through impact. But a bent left knee at and after impact stops this powerful releasing movement. Make five practice swings with your right hand only.

Place your left hand on your left hip. As you swing down and through, let your left hand push your left hip out of the way. Feel your left leg straighten as you do this. When you get used to this move, work it into your full-speed action.

AS USED BY... DAVIS LOVE III

People wonder where this beanpole American gets his amazing power from. It's down to his left leg position which gives a free, powerful turn through the ball.

Set up to fit the slope

Great places, driving ranges – every lie is perfectly flat. On an average golf course though, you will make at least half your swings with the ball above or below your feet, yet these are shots you rarely get to practise. The most common error golfers make is trying to address the ball as they would for a level-lie shot. This leads to a swing that fights the contours rather than flows with them. Here are a few straightforward set-up and swing rules that help you use the slope instead of fighting it.

1: BALL ABOVE YOUR FEET

Remember the spin

This lie will put hookspin on the ball, causing it to spin to the left for a right-hander. Imagine a ball dropped on a slope to remember this. The ball will always spin the way it bounces.

Counter the spin

Aim 10 yards right of target to counter spin. Ensure your feet, hips and shoulders aim parallel to this line. The steeper the slope, the more spin you will create so aim further right.

Add flex to your knees

The slope will send your weight back to your heels. Counter this by flexing your knees until your weight moves forward to the balls of your feet. The height of the ball will force you to set up with a more upright spine angle. Be aware you will make a flatter swing because of it.

Hold down the grip

The relative height of the ball reduces the distance between your shoulders and clubhead. Compensate by holding the club a little further down the grip than usual. The more severe the sideslope, the further down you should grip.

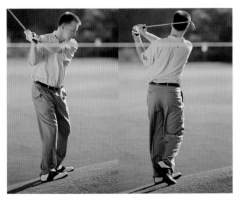

Flatter swing, back and through

The lie and your almost vertical spine will encourage a more rotary action. Your hands should not get much above shoulder height back and through. Contrast this with a level lie, where your hands will end up pretty much above your right shoulder at the top of the backswing and above the left shoulder at the end of the followthrough.

Visualize the spin

You can confidently expect the ball to slice from this lie (spin to the right for a right-hander). Again, remember this rule by visualizing a ball dropped on the slope. The ball spins the way that it runs.

Make the club as long as possible

Use all of the grip while making sure the heel of your hand can put pressure on top of the handle. You want to make the club as long as possible while retaining total control over it.

Aim left of target

Feet, hips and shoulders should aim left of the hole. These dictate the line the ball starts on, and you must start the ball left to allow for the cutspin this lie will cause. Place a club across your body to gain a feel for your aim. As with the ball above your feet, aim further off-line as the slope becomes more severe.

Bend more

The distance between your shoulders and the ball is now further than usual, so you must bend more to get down to the ball. Bend more from your hips. This puts your spine on a sharper angle. Try to keep your spine fairly straight as you do it. Don't be afraid to stick your rear out; if you just hunch your back to get down to the ball you will only straighten up through the shot, as well as risking serious stress to your spine.

Flex your knees more than normal. As well as getting you lower, this helps you to balance, compensating for having to bend.

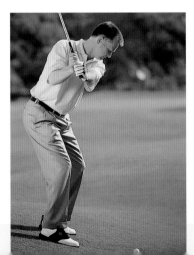

◀Upright backswing

Your posture will cause an upright swing. You will feel the shaft almost vertical halfway into the backswing. This steep angle will help you get the clubhead down to the ball.

Learn to swing out-of-balance

Unless you play on dead flat courses, it's vital to be able to hit the ball cleanly off all kinds of slopes. Upslopes and downslopes tend to throw you off balance and make good ball striking a lot harder. Many golfers are unsure how to balance themselves while making a full swing from such lies. Correct preparation and understanding how the slope affects the flight of the ball are the key to success.

1: PLAYING OFF DOWNSLOPES

 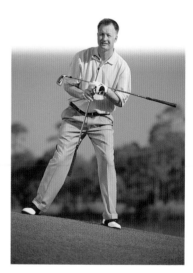

Move the ball back in your stance:

Play the ball behind centre in your stance. This helps you make a clean strike on the back of the ball, not always an easy job when the ground behind it is higher. Move the ball further back as the slope becomes steeper, but never play it outside your back foot.

Lean with the slope:

Lean forward (left shoulder towards the target for right-handers) at set-up. Aim to get your spine forming a 90° angle with the slope. Imagine there are cross-hairs between the ground and your spine – it will help you form that right angle. Your shoulder line should mirror the gradient.

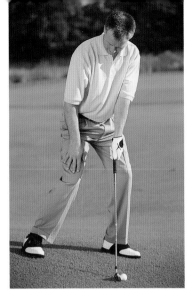

Soften your back knee:

Of course, leaning towards the target will put more weight on to your left side. In order to compensate for this, balance yourself by adding some flex to your back knee.

Make a steep backswing:

Allow the clubhead to rise sharply away from the ground. This may produce a slightly upright backswing but will help you make the steeply angled downswing you need to strike the ball and not the turf.

Chase the slope:

Try to make the clubhead hug the ground through impact and beyond. The only way you will make a clean strike from a downhill lie is with a throughswing that really follows the contours of the ground. Don't worry if you lose your balance toppling forward; I'd rather see you do that than fall back on to your right side – a surefire recipe for a duff.

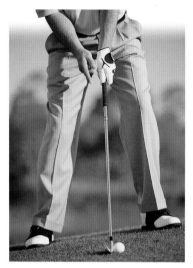

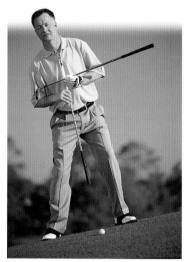

Move the ball forward in your stance:

This encourages you to swing up the hill with the slope, so avoiding the risk of chopping into the ground. Never play the ball further forward than opposite your left toe-cap.

Spine at right angles to slope:

Again imagine those crosshairs, your spine lined up with one and the slope in line with the other. This involves dropping your right shoulder and leaning away from your target.

ON-COURSE CHECKPOINT

BALL POSITIONING: Move ball position towards the higher foot, whether you're hitting uphill or downhill; in other words forward for upslopes and back for downslopes.

TARGET LINE

Aim right of target:

Upslopes can tend to make you pull the ball, so aim a few yards right of the target. Aim further right as the upslope becomes more severe.

CHECKPOINT

WEIGHT FORWARD ON THE THROUGHSWING: Gravity will tend to throw you on to your back foot at address and through the swing, leading to huge pull-hooks. Practice swings will build the feeling of your weight moving forward up the slope.

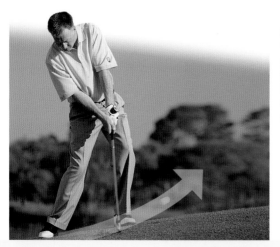

Let your swing follow the contours:

Keep the club low to the ground on the way back. Again, aim to let the clubhead follow the slope contours.

Distance control is the key to getting up and down

If you think that the difference between hitting the ball 40 yards and 50 yards is some kind of instinctive, elusive adjustment to your feel and touch, you are wrong. There are solid, easy-to-learn methods that will enable you to add or take away power to your shot at will. We are going to look at four common situations where distance control is vital – a short bunker shot, a putt, a pitch and when you are in-between clubs – and for each I will show you how to apply these techniques.

Focus on followthrough

Normally you would look at your backswing to control distance, but I will show you why adjusting your followthrough is better. Change the length of your throughswing by taking control of your chest. Pivot your chest to different positions to hit different lengths of shot.

1: PERFECT PITCHING

Focus on your chest to control the distance on pitch shots from 25–75 yards.

From 25 yards out

Turn your chest just past square. Keep your hands and club in front of your breastbone.

AS USED BY... **NICK PRICE**

Nick tops the scrambling stats, getting up and down 67.5% of the time. Take every opportunity to watch his pitching technique, and how his hands and arms work in perfect ratio to his pivoting chest.

From 50 yards out

Simply pivot through a little further, chest almost facing your target. Again, take care to keep your hands bang in front of your turning torso.

From 75 yards out

Turn your body through until your chest looks at the hole, hands and club once more in front of your body. Here that means clubshaft pointing at your target.

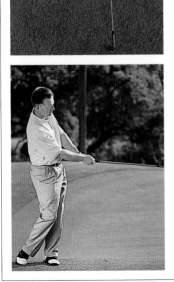

2: SHORT TRAP SHOT

Dictate how far you hit the ball by controlling and adjusting the length of your followthrough position.

Reduce followthrough

Aim to hit the sand a couple of inches behind the ball, as usual, but hold your followthrough with your hands at waist height. This keeps you from building up too much pace in the downswing and at impact.

Adjust the followthrough

Work on this position by imagining the butt of your sand wedge is pointing at your belt buckle. With experience, you will learn to follow through a little past your belt buckle for a slightly longer shot, and a little lower than the buckle for a shorter shot.

Three-quarters back

Make a three-quarter backswing, hands to shoulder height, back facing the target, and your weight balanced evenly on both feet.

Quick tip

With tight pin positions, make an honest assessment of your ability to get close. Your priority is to get the ball out, so you are better 10 feet past and putting than 10 feet short and splashing out again.

3: BETWEEN CLUBS

Always take the more powerful club (eg an 8-iron instead of a 9) and take a little bit off it. Here are three ways to do that.

STEP 1: Choke down the grip...
Leave an inch gap between the top of your higher hand and the butt of the grip. Shortening the club like this reduces the arc of your swing, which cuts down the power.

STEP 2: Make a quieter turn...
Stop swinging back as soon as you see your left shoulder. This is a shorter turn than you would normally make. Again, this cuts back on the force of impact while giving you more control over the shot.

STEP 3: Three-quarter throughswing... Make an effort to keep your followthrough shorter than usual. Visualize yourself finishing as I have here – in perfect balance, with hands at head height and club pointing skyward. You do not need to pound the ball; the straighter-faced club will ensure the ball flies all the way back to the pin.

Length of stroke and grip pressure are the keys that can unlock your putting touch.

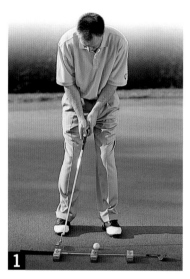

Make it a pendulum

STEP 1: Aim a clubshaft at the hole. Place three golf-ball boxes along its shaft, a foot between each, as shown. Position a golf ball opposite the middle ball box and set up to it, using your normal putting address position. Make a backswing long enough to take the putter head opposite the rear box.

STEP 2: Now follow through until the putter head is opposite the holeside box. Swinging back and through the same amount is your first step to regulating the pace of the ball. This is what is meant when pros refer to a 'pendulum' stroke. Simply increase the pendulum swing as the putt gets longer.

PUTTING CHECKPOINT

SOFT HANDS: Hold the putter lightly in your hands. Soft hands help you feel the putter head and give you more feel – vital if you're going to gauge putts correctly.

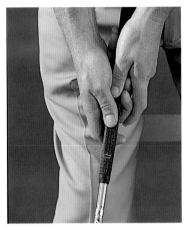

Short putts – wrists firm

Look at the back of your right wrist. Make sure the angle in the back of your right wrist stays constant through this short stroke. This lack of wrist movement will help you keep the putter head square, crucial on short putts where accuracy is key.

Long putts – wrists give

Again, focus on the back of your right wrist. Let it hinge a little on the backswing. It will help you generate the power to cover the distance to the hole. As you follow through, allow the right wrist to release so its back is almost flat. This flexibility helps your touch, too.

Smarten up your short game to score

How many greens in regulation do you think Ernie Els hits over 18 holes? 16? 17? In fact the answer is 12. The official PGA Tour stats reveal Ernie hit just 64.4% of greens for the 2002 season. That equates to around six greens missed a round, yet he still managed to shoot well under par regularly! Even Tiger Woods, who topped the GIR list, misses one out of every four greens he aims at. Such statistics prove to us that scoring isn't about hitting the green so much as what happens when you miss it. Top pros can turn three shots into two all day long because they have razor-sharp chipping and pitching skills and are great out of sand. I am going to focus on these three areas and pass on some of their secrets.

1: CHIPPING – ONE ACTION, DIFFERENT CLUBS

Missing the green can leave you with many types of chip shot, but do not alter your technique for each one. Instead, learn one chipping action and simply alter the club you use. Split chip shots into different carry and roll ratios depending on how much green you have to work with.

SHORT CHIP 1
75% carry, 25% run: SW

MEDIUM CHIP 2
50% carry, 50% run: 9-iron

LONG CHIP 3
25% carry, 75% run: 7-iron

Whichever club you play you must strike the ball cleanly, ensuring you do not hit turf before the ball. A downward strike is the best way to achieve this. Address the ball to promote a descending blow.

Grip down to the metal

This gives your hands greater feel and control of the clubhead. 'Shortening' the club like this also takes some power out, allowing you to hit the ball firmly.

Push your left forearm forward

It should form a line with the clubshaft. This helps you move your hands forward of the ball, again leading to a crisp downward strike.

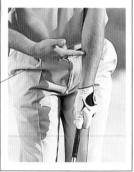

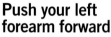

Feet close together

Keep them perhaps a clubhead's length apart. You want to minimize body movement on this shot. A narrow stance limits body action whereas a wider stance, and increased stability, gives your body more licence to move.

Weight favours front foot

This will encourage a downward hit on to the back of the ball and avoid that dreaded 'flub'.

Again, simply work on one chipping action for all clubs. The different lofts on the clubface will send the ball different lengths and trajectories.

Hinge your right wrist

As you swing back, focus on the back of your right wrist. Make sure it feels soft enough to increase its hinge. This adds feel to your hands and steepens the angle of attack.

Keep the 'Y' shape

Your two arms and clubshaft should create a Y shape at address. Keep that right through to your finishing position to help you avoid flicking at the ball with your hands.

Check the left

When you reach the end of your followthrough, hold the position. Check that your left arm and clubshaft are still in line.

Hit down

Hit down on the ball, as if you were trying to trap it between the clubhead and the ground. Aim to take a scraping divot – no more, no less.

First things first, we sometimes say, and when chipping we need, before doing anything else, to know how far we are likely to hit the ball. Unless you can gauge that correctly, you will always struggle with your short game.

Know your length

There's no point worrying about technique until you know your yardages. You would not expect to look good in clothes without knowing your measurements, so how can you expect to hit the ball close when you don't know how far your swing will send the ball?

You will only pitch the ball consistently close when you know the length of swing needed to send it the right distance. The only place to learn this is on the practice ground. Spend some time learning how far your hip-to-hip swing, or shoulder-to shoulder swing, sends the ball.

100 YARDS

75 YARDS

50 YARDS

2: MOVE ARMS AND BODY TOGETHER

It is vital when chipping to synchronize the movement of your arms and body. Get this wrong and the shot will almost certainly turn out wrong too. Here is a simple drill to help reinforce the correct technique.

Turn in sync

Grip your wedge in your right hand and hold a clubshaft across your chest with the left.

Make five practice swings, making sure your body turn responds in sync to your arm swing. The longer you swing, the more you turn; the shorter, the less. If your body does not turn with your arms you will hit fats, thins and off-line shots.

As your arm swing lengthens, so should your body turn increase. Keep everything synchronized.

AS USED BY... **LEE TREVINO**

Lee Trevino was a short hitter but a great scorer. He would spend hours working on his pitching. He once said, 'These days you can drive up to the average golf club and see three dinosaurs for every golfer working on their pitch-and-run shots.'

Beat bunker nightmares

Sand shots are hard enough when you have a perfect lie and level stance. But sadly the nature of bunkers – i.e. huge holes in the ground that collect water – means you are often having to play off strange slopes and even stranger lies. We are going to look at four common tricky situations that bunkers can throw up, and I will show you the simplest way to play each one. In each case success depends on adjusting not just your swing but also your set-up. Do not ignore the set-up tips – they make the swing you will need to produce much easier to achieve.

NIGHTMARE 1: | SEVERE UPSLOPE

This slope sends the ball high into the air with no run at all. The difficulty here is in getting the ball back to the hole. You must thump your sand wedge into the sand aggressively for a rising shot that travels to the hole through the air and stops quickly on landing.

1: BUILD YOUR SET-UP

1 BACK LEG STRAIGHT: Straighten your back leg to anchor yourself in the sand. It gives you a base to swing from. Hips and shoulders follow the sand contours.

2 CLUBFACE SQUARE: For a traditional sand shot you will open the face (aim it right of target) to add loft. But the upslope here already gives you a very high launch angle for the shot. The biggest difficulty is getting the ball up to the hole, so square the face up.

3 BALL FORWARD OF CENTRE: You need for this shot to drive hard into the sand behind the ball. Moving the ball forward in your stance helps you do this, making it easier for you to hit sand before the ball.

2: SWING – SHORT AND SHARP

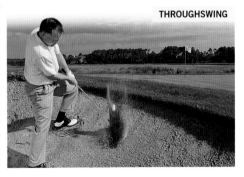

BACKSWING

THROUGHSWING

Test your backswing

Your wide stance will restrict your backswing. If you try to swing back fully you run the risk of overbalancing. Make a couple of practice backswings to feel the length you can make without losing your posture and stability.

Hit the sand hard

Thump the sand aggressively, just behind the ball. The shockwaves caused by the clubhead hitting the sand force the ball up and out. The upslope sends the ball up, not forwards; don't worry about hitting it too far.

The bank of sand high behind the ball makes it very hard for you to swing the clubhead into the sand and under the ball. You must lean with the slope to alter your swing's angle of attack and allow the clubhead to bite down into the sand. Expect a low, running result.

Quick tip

For this shot, there are two things to remember: 1) Trust the loft on the club to get the ball over the lip; don't try to help it. 2) The sharper you strike down, the more you help the ball to rise.

Lean with the slope

Lean so your shoulders and hips are parallel to the slope. This will help you swing the clubhead into the sand and under the ball. You will feel more weight on your left foot – that's fine. Keep your knees evenly flexed to help your balance.

1: BUILD YOUR SET-UP

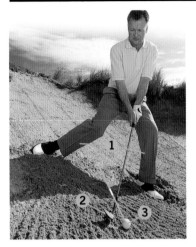

1 **WIDEN YOUR FEET:** A wider stance not only gives you better stability – it also lowers your upper body, which helps you strike the sand before the ball.

2 **AIM THE CLUBFACE WIDE OF THE TARGET:** The ball will come out lower than normal from a downhill lie. You need the extra loft of an open face to beat the bunker lip in front of you.

3 **PLAY THE BALL JUST BEHIND CENTRE IN YOUR STANCE:** This gives you the best angle of attack into the ball while helping you hit the ball up and over the lip. As with any such shot, set-up is as important as swing.

2: SWING – STEEP, THEN FOLLOW THE SAND

BACKSWING

THROUGHSWING

Make it steep
Pick the club up sharply, with plenty of wrist action. This is vital if you are to make the sharp, downward action you need to strike into the sand behind the ball. Your correct set-up will make this easier to achieve.

Follow the slope
Keep the clubhead as low to the sand as you can on the way through. You are sunk if you try to help the ball up into the air. Keep your knees flexed to help yourself stay down through the stroke.

It only takes a few grains of sand to turn a towering fairway trap shot into a humiliating 20-yard flub. Effective fairway bunker technique is all aimed at striking the ball cleanly, perhaps even a little thin. Use your set-up and maintain your height to nip the ball cleanly.

1: BUILD YOUR SET-UP

1 DON'T BURY YOUR FEET: Many golfers wriggle their feet into the sand automatically. Avoid doing this for long trap shots because it lowers you in the sand and makes you more likely to hit sand before ball.

2 BALL JUST FORWARD OF CENTRE: You want the club to neither rise nor fall as it sweeps through the ball. The position shown is perfect for promoting such a strike.

3 TENSE YOUR FOREARMS: This shortens your swing and cuts down on wrist action, making your strike less powerful but more accurate. Take extra club to make up for loss of power.

4 GRIP DOWN THE CLUB AN INCH: This 'shortens' the club, which gives you a better chance of striking the ball cleanly.

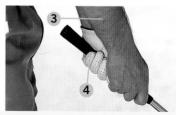

Palm under chin

Visualize swinging with your palm under your chin. This helps you develop the feeling of maintaining your height through the swing. Many golfers ruin their chances of a good shot by sagging or dipping through the ball – a surefire recipe for disaster.

Keep it compact

You can easily slip if you try to hit the ball too hard so keep your action three-quarter length. This keeps your swing compact – vital if you are to make the accurate strike this shot needs. Compensate for the length this will take off the shot by playing a less-lofted club.

Quick tip

For long bunker shots your divot should be very shallow, the club just skimming the sand. A good way to visualize this is to think of the divot as a thin slice of ham, rather than the usual fillet of steak.

Usually you get this shot after heavy rain, when the sodden sand takes on the consistency of concrete. Forget traditional bunker technique here and play the shot with a chipping action.

1: BUILD YOUR SET-UP

1 BALL POSITION BACK: Play the ball back in your stance – just inside your right heel is perfect. This pre-sets the downward strike you need off this lie.

2 STANCE NARROW: This is a shot that needs great precision in the strike. By narrowing your stance you cut down on body movement, helping you keep your head still and your strike accurate.

3 WEIGHT FORWARD: Favour your left side with your weight. Again, this encourages a downward strike on to the back of the ball. The last thing you need here is to catch the sand first.

AS USED BY... SEVE BALLESTEROS

The Spaniard has been one if the finest exponents of these shots His secret, was keeping body movement to a minimum off hard sand.

Keep it short

The ball will come out fast and low, so keep the backswing as short as for a traditional chip shot, using a hands-and-arms action.

Keep it equal

Keep your backswing and throughswing equal in length. This stops you getting flicky through the ball.

BACKSWING

THROUGHSWING

Impact

By moving the ball back in your stance you have automatically placed your hands ahead of the clubhead at set-up. Keep this relationship as you strike the ball, hands leading the club through the ball.

Divot check

1: This would be the typical sand divot for a traditional bunker shot. The ball is in the middle of the sand you take.
2: With the shot off a firm lie, you should move the ball to the beginning of your sand divot, as you would for a normal fairway shot.

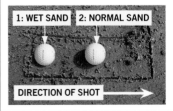

1: WET SAND   2: NORMAL SAND

DIRECTION OF SHOT

SHORT SHOTS – THINK STEEP

On short trap shots you need the ball to rise and fall quickly. A steep angle of attack into the ball will give you that trajectory – imagine the clubhead describing a saucer shape through impact.

Shirt buttons ahead of the ball

Feel more weight go on to your front foot and knee. This helps lean your chest forward, promoting that steep angle of attack and transferring more energy down into the sand.

Make a steep, sharp backswing

Feel the clubhead rise quickly away from the sand. Don't be afraid to get your hands and wrists involved to help you make this sharp backswing.

Quick tip

Your mind finds it much easier to focus on images than words. Keep the saucer image in your head, and use similar images for other shots you find problematic.

Spank the sand hard

Hit down sharply into the sand behind the ball. You'll find this a lot easier after the set-up and backswing changes you have made. The abrupt angle of attack will pop the ball up quickly and softly, perfect for a short bunker shot.

LONG SHOTS – THINK SWEEP

A shallower swing will help the ball come out on a flatter trajectory. This time, imagine a dinner-plate angle of attack rather than the saucer you wanted for the short shot.

Buttons behind the ball

Keep your weight even on both feet. Drop your right knee a touch so that you lean a little away from the hole. This promotes a shallower angle of attack, which helps you hit the ball further.

Make a wide shallow backswing

This time keep the clubhead lower to the sand for longer during the takeaway. It will help you produce the wide, shallow attack needed to hit the ball those extra yards.

Complete your throughswing

Instead of hitting down into the sand, work on skimming the ball forward. Swing to a long, full followthrough. You must follow through on all trap shots, but on long bunker shots you can go through that bit further.

Banish your golfing myths

There is no sport like golf for misinformation. Maybe it's because the game is so hard to play well that there is so much well-intentioned advice flying about. The trouble is that a lot of it does more harm than good. This section will help you identify and banish the most common and damaging splats of so-called golfing advice, in each case offering a far better course of action to follow. It will give you an improved understanding of the mechanics of your swing and what you are trying to achieve on each and every shot.

MYTH 1: 'SHIFT YOUR WEIGHT'

The problem

Most golfers know they should get their weight on to their back foot and behind the ball at the top of the backswing but as soon as they attempt this they are sunk. Hips lunge sideways and weight rocks to the outside of the back foot. There's no balance and no power.

Turn your weight

STEP 1: Stick an umbrella six inches outside your back foot, in line with your back leg. With your right hand, hold your 5-iron by the head against the front of your left shoulder. Aim the shaft at your target. Keep your weight even on both feet.

STEP 2: Turn slowly and smoothly with your shoulders, keeping the clubhead and shaft against your left shoulder. Keep the shaft level with the ground as you turn.

STEP 3: Keep the clubhead against your left shoulder. As you turn, make sure your back leg holds its position. It must not get any closer to your brolly than it was at your starting position. As you complete your turn you will feel yourself wound up powerfully with your weight 'turned' over a flexed back leg. This is the key to effective weight transfer.

Hold that position

Watch out for the shaft dropping so it points to the ground, and your right hip moving towards the umbrella. This is your old 'shift-your-weight' position. Make sure the shaft stays horizontal and your right hip holds its position.

The problem

If you try to return to your address position at impact you will hit all manner of powerless duffs. You will not be able to swing through powerfully to your target, and you will hit a lot of thin shots because the clubhead will be rising at impact instead of descending.

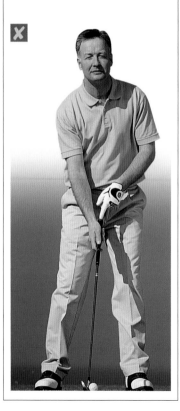

AT ADDRESS: Your shaft is almost vertical, leaning a little forward so that the grip end is a fraction nearer the hole than the head.

AT IMPACT: You need a downward strike to transfer maximum power into the ball. Hands need to be well ahead of the ball.

Learn the two key differences:

Hip position

AT ADDRESS: Your hips are square to your target line – not aiming at your target but towards a point parallel left of it.

AT IMPACT: The force you need to generate means a clubshaft across your hips would aim well left.

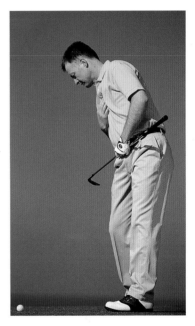

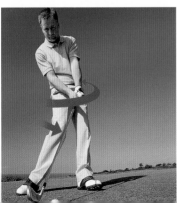

Shaft angle

You also need your left hip out of the way to give your hands and arms room to swing through the ball. Achieve this by allowing your right knee to move forward with the swinging club. This simple move allows your left hip to turn smoothly to the left.

The problem

A clubshaft that parallels the ground may look neat and orthodox, but it has wrongly come to represent a full backswing. Instead, all you really need to think about achieving is a 90° wrist hinge and shoulder turn.

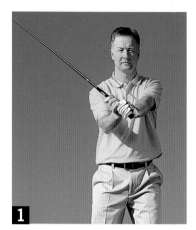

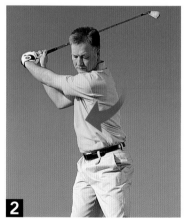

Try the 45° drill

STEP 1: Hold the club in front of you, hands bang in front of your chest. Angle the shaft so it runs up at a 45° angle, or through your right shoulder.

STEP 2: Turn your chest as much as possible. Keep your hands in front of your chest as you go. When your shoulders can turn no more, this is your full backswing. It does not matter whether the clubshaft is parallel or not.

AS USED BY... **TIGER WOODS**

Tiger's clubshaft does not always reach horizontal, but no one would accuse him of having an incomplete backswing. Look at the huge shoulder turn and wrist hinge. Take a leaf out of Tiger's book and forget about shaft position at the top.

The problem

Almost every topped shot is blamed on lifting your head, but 9 out of 10 golfers never do so. Forcing your head down freezes your body, which then obstructs your arms and prevents them swinging through. You end up making a scooping action through the ball, the very thing that leads to a top.

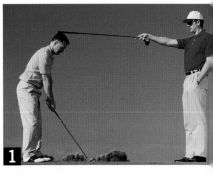

Keep your height

Avoid dropping your head. Retain your height until after you've struck the ball.

Stand tall through impact

STEP 1: Set up to a ball. Ask a friend to stand opposite you and rest the grip of a golf club gently on top of your head.

STEP 2: Hit the shot, making sure your head does not drop down from the shaft at impact. You will find it much easier to get the club down to the bottom of the ball when you give your hands and arms a constant base to push away from.

It sounds logical that if you swing straight through the ball with a square clubface the ball will fly straight. But in fact it leads to a wooden, powerless impact position. The circular nature of a correct swing means the clubhead travels in a gently rounded arc and only rotates back to square briefly through impact.

WRONG
Square face = weak slices

CORRECT
Clubface rotates

Trying to hold the face square at impact is counterproductive and usually causes a slice.

1

2

Feel the club

STEP 1: Take your 9-iron and grip down almost to the metal with your right hand only. Hold your right elbow against your side with your left hand. Make a half backswing, ensuring your left hand holds your right elbow close to your side. Feel how the clubface rotates naturally from its start position to a point where its toe-end points at the target.

STEP 2: Now reverse things. Grip the club in your left hand and hold your left elbow against your side with your right hand. Swing through to a half-followthrough position, again taking care to keep your left elbow against your side. This time, feel how the clubhead turns naturally with the swinging motion to a point where its toe points away from the target.

MIND**Z**ONE

Technique is vital in golf but it's not everything, for the game involves the mind as well as body – as increasingly recognized by top players. Negative thoughts can destroy a round, your skills counting for nothing if you cannot produce the goods when it matters. Renowned sports psychologist Karl Morris shows how to harness your thoughts and feelings so that they work for rather than against you and reveals how visualization and self-awareness can help improve your game.

Work from home!

You can improve your golf without setting foot anywhere near the course. If you doubt this, listen to the story of Captain Gerald Coffee. The American was shot down during the Vietnam war and spent seven years imprisoned in North Vietnam. Coffee retained his sanity by mentally playing the perfect round on his home golf course, day after day. After release, Coffee went to his course and played almost exactly the round he had envisioned – his personal best by far. Similarly, people have been shown to grow physically stronger merely by imagining they are lifting weights. In other words visualization is an important tool in your practice box of tricks.

RELAX AND ENJOY

Relax yourself. Sit down somewhere quiet, where you know you won't be disturbed. A state of relaxation allows you to visualize as clearly as possible.

Picture your perfect swing

Imagine you are watching a movie of yourself swinging the club. Picture yourself making your best swing possible and hitting a great shot. Make your imagery as vivid as possible by using your senses.

SIGHT: What colour shirt are you wearing? How green is the grass? How blue is the sky? How does your shirt crease as you turn? What does your finishing position look like? Who are you playing with? What are they wearing?

HEARING: Are the birds singing? What noise do your clothes make as you stretch and turn? How does impact sound? What do your playing partners say to you after you have hit the perfect shot?

FEEL: How does the wind or sun feel on your face? How does the club feel in your hands? What sensation do you feel as your shirt brushes your chin when you complete your turn? How do your arms feel as you swing through to a perfect followthrough?

AS USED BY... **GARY PLAYER**

When the South African legend got to the 1965 US Open at Bellerive, he visualized his name in gold letters at the top of the leaderboard. He went on to win the fourth of his nine Majors.

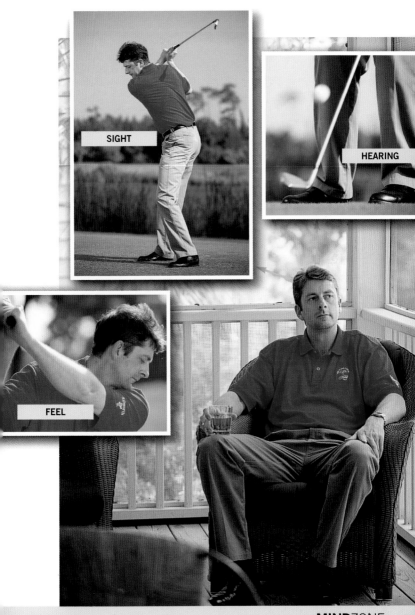

SIGHT

HEARING

FEEL

Picture yourself playing the course

Put yourself in a position on the course where you struggle – perhaps a long putt or a tricky bunker shot. See yourself playing the shot successfully. It will build positive emotions and feelings that will give you confidence next time you find yourself in that position.

Use a mirror

If you have trouble forming a crystal-clear image of your swing, try making it in front of a mirror. Rehearse the positions you find troublesome – maybe the takeaway, or change of direction at the top. Build for yourself a clear visual representation of the position, one that you can recall instantly when you're out on the course and need to make a good swing.

Swing with eyes closed

Make a slow-motion, eyes-closed swing. Focus on your senses – how does it feel? Which top pro's action does it look most like? This builds feel by improving your body's ability to do what your mind is telling it.

Ingrain new moves

Your muscles can only remember one new move at a time. You may come away from a lesson with several new moves to build into your swing, but if you work on them all at once you will not build up the necessary connections from brain to muscle to make that move permanent and automatic. The move gets lost.

Quick tip

Always remember the swing is fluid and you are swinging *through* positions, not *to* them. Aim to ingrain a movement rather than a static position. Visualize this until it becomes second nature.

One thing at a time

Use your time at home to allow one new move to sink in. Let your mind focus on that move and that move alone for at least six hours after a lesson. It's a little like waiting for a jelly to set – it will, as long as you wait long enough!

Work on one new position at a time... ...work on two at once and you'll lose both.

Start before the round

The time from closing the front door to arriving on the first tee is important – it can have you striking your first tee shot as anything from a jittery, nervous wreck to the very definition of relaxed and confident. It is personal preference how long your preparation takes you, but do make your pre-round actions a matter of routine. I often see golfers arrive at the course 15 minutes before their tee time week

Play music on the way to the course

Music is a terrific mood-setter. It's great for influencing your state of mind – how much exercise would you get done at the gym if they played Beethoven instead of rock music? So play some tunes that will help put you in your optimum state of mind. And it does not have to be soft, bland supermarket music. If you play your best golf while in a quiet, dreamy state of mind, put on some mild ambient or acoustic stuff. If you're at your best when playing a powerful, aggressive game, play some loud, upbeat rock music – anything that gets you in the mood.

AS USED BY...
JACK NICKLAUS

'I do a lot of humming on the course,' said Jack once. 'I tend to stick with the same song; I once shot a 66 to Moon River.'

in, week out, and then suddenly arrive an hour earlier for the club championship. They end up putting extra pressure on themselves and throwing their rhythms out. It leads to disjointed thinking and swinging. You do not have to set out for the course hours ahead of your tee time – in fact you can use the tips I give here in just 15 minutes – but whatever your preference, keep it the same every time.

Putt balls to a small coin

This alters your perception of the size of the hole. On good putting days the hole always looks bigger; on bad putting days it looks minuscule. Putting to a coin gives you a tiny target, compared to which the hole looks cavernous. It also puts you in a win-win situation. If you miss the coin it does not feel like failure because you know how small your target is. Your mind does not register it as a miss. Compare this to putting at a hole and missing, which can put a serious dent in your confidence.

Drink water, avoid coffee

Caffeine in coffee is a stimulant. It may be good for keeping you awake when the Masters is on, but forget it before a round of golf. Your body is usually already at a high state of awareness and anxiety and you don't need anything that turns the levels up even more. Drinks like coffee and cola will also give you a short-term energy boost, from which you will come down a few holes later. It makes it harder to be consistent in your swinging and your thinking. Instead, drink water. It keeps you hydrated and will not mess around with your energy levels.

Putting ladder

It's vital you register a sense of feel in those few minutes you grab on the practice green. Always play at least one putting ladder game. Take five balls and knock the first 20 feet away. Aim to knock the second 15 feet, the third 10 feet and so on. It gives you a sense of touch that you would not garner if you putted at the holes, when how close you come to holing the ball becomes the object of your focus.

Swing with three clubs

This helps you smoothen your swing – nobody ever swung three clubs in a jerky fashion. It also loosens up your muscles and helps them relax.

Quick tip

A consistent routine before you start is as important as the round itself. Get your mind and body relaxed, full of positive thoughts, and you're already well on the way to shooting a good score.

Make your own commitment card

Before each round I want you to get into the habit of writing down three or four instructions on a card for the round to come. These instructions are the mental commitments you will stick to for 18 holes. They should cover areas of the game where you struggle – perhaps 'Stay in the present' if your mind happens to wander forward or back, 'Take 10 deep breaths from the stomach' if you tend to get nervous, or 'Keep your eyes above the horizon' for those who get down and introspective.

Read your commitments before you start and again at the turn. After you finish, have a look at the list again and give yourself a mark out of 10 for how well you kept to each one. Any for which you score less than eight should be on your card for the next round.

Control the controllables

You will play your best golf when your state of mind is calm and positive. Yet during the course of 18 holes there are any number of incidents waiting to throw you off an even keel. The problem is that many golfers allow things to get to them that they cannot do anything

The weather

A well-struck putt is blown off-line by a gust of wind. You can rant at the situation or you can take it on the chin, grasping that the missed putt had nothing to do with your technique or execution. Providing you are mortal, the natural elements are, quite simply, out of your control.

So... rather than wasting energy complaining and shaking your fist at the elements, accept that the conditions are equally difficult for everyone.

The ball

As much as you would like to think you can control the ball, the plain fact is you can't. You can influence it, and some golfers influence it better than others. But however good you are, you can flub a chip or slice into the bushes any time.

So... give yourself a break if you hit a bad shot. As long as you have given it your best, to beat yourself up is of no value to you whatsoever. Put it behind you and approach the next shot on its merits.

about. You will be happier on the course when you learn to stop letting whatever you can't control affect you. Here is a guide to help you identify those things you can do something about and those things you should waste no time fretting over.

Your opponent

Your opponent may suddenly develop a hot putter and start holing putts from all over the green. Many golfers lose patience or curse their luck at drawing this player on such a good day. Doing so, however, will only make you play worse and will have no effect on what your opponent does.

So... get it into your head that you can do nothing about it. Applaud your opponent's good play and hope their hot streak ends.

The course

You nail a drive up the middle, only to find it in a deep divot. Okay, you wouldn't be human if you didn't experience some annoyance. But keep it in perspective. Nobody can guarantee that such ill luck will never happen.

So... feel your annoyance, then let it go. You have a hard shot to play, and you need all your concentration for it. Fretting over your bad fortune is the best way to turn a bit of bad luck into a high score.

The reactions

You have a choice about how to react to a missed short putt, or any other bad shot. You can either hurl your ball furiously into the nearest bush or pond, or you can keep a lid on it and give yourself a massive boost when it comes to making cool and sensible decisions on the next tee.

Your attitude

You can walk on to the tee like a dormouse or a lion. If you choose the first option you will give yourself and everyone else the impression that you don't really want to be there and that you're trying to get the whole thing over as quickly as possible. Your chances of hitting a good shot are far better if you announce yourself confidently on the tee. Get your chin up and keep your movements brisk and purposeful.

Your routines

Developing and sticking to a pre-shot routine gives you an advantage when it comes to being consistent. It gives your game a rhythm, ensures you take all factors into account and stops you hitting the ball before you are ready. Whether or not you do this is entirely within your control. All top players do so – you should too.

AS USED BY... **JUSTIN ROSE**

Watch the young Englishman on the course and you'll see how disciplined he is about going through the same pre-shot routine before every shot. Justin never plays before he's ready – a sound lesson from which every amateur can benefit.

Your effort

You are in direct control of how much effort you put in at all times on the course. It's easy to miss a tap-in by not making the effort to line it up properly. By making sure you grind out 100% at all times, you will bring your scores down and gain more respect for yourself as a golfer. Both of these will give you more confidence.

Quick tip

Attempting to change what's outside your control will hinder rather than help your game. Focus instead on changing what you *can* control – above all, yourself.

Stop the scorecard changing your game

Put a scorecard in a golfer's hand and his whole attitude changes. Suddenly he starts playing shots he wouldn't normally play, either over-safe or over-aggressive. He stops thinking about the next shot and instead worries about the stroke index one hole up ahead, or the three-putt on the previous green. He starts to brood about his lack of touch and confidence. He spends the whole round preoccupied by how he is doing. In short, he stops enjoying himself. In what follows are some ways to deal with these common mind glitches, including: how to keep your mind on the present, how to feel more confident on the first green and how to stop becoming preoccupied with your score. Put these tactics into play and you will start enjoying your golf again, even with a scorecard in your back pocket.

1: BUILD CONFIDENCE – PRACTISE PUTTING

I often see golfers working on their stroke before going out to play a match. But it's too late then to work on mechanics – you will only become over-aware of your stroke on the course. Instead, work on feel and confidence with holing out.

Touch: putt from fringe to fringe

When you are working on touch it is vital you take the hole out of the equation. You will only get caught up in trying to sink the ball. Instead, simply set up on the fringe of the green and roll six balls to the opposite fringe. It's a great way of establishing feel in your hands as well as gauging the pace of the greens.

Accuracy:
putt to a tee peg

Instead of putting to a hole, stick a tee peg in the green and roll some five-footers towards it. If you hit the tee peg you will get a buzz from hitting such an accurate putt; if you miss it, you can tell yourself the ball would have dropped in a hole. Either way you suffer no loss of confidence from seeing yourself miss putts.

Putting to a tee peg alters your perception of the size of the hole, which suddenly looks like a big target to you when you reach the first green. Once again, it's all a question of the mind.

AS USED BY... **JACK NICKLAUS**

When Nicklaus was asked about how to practise putting, he said, 'You gotta dance with the lady who brung you.' In other words, it's too late to work on your stroke. Work on your confidence and feel instead.

3RD GEAR
Take the shot on.

1ST GEAR
Play safe.

Get in gear

Much poor scoring is down to poor decision-making, and poor decision-making is often caused by not paying attention to how well you are playing. When you reach the 3rd tee, give your game a 'gear' for how well you are playing: 1st gear means damage limitation; 2nd is average; 3rd means you can flow along, going with how you feel. For the rest of the round, make your course-management decisions for the gear you are in. Too many players make 3rd-gear decisions when their game is only in 1st.

Quick tip

Avoid a damage-limitation 1st-gear day by imagining your swing is being marked on artistic impression. Focus on two areas – a smooth transition at the top, and a balanced finish.

Don't look down

Pay attention to where you are looking as you walk up the fairway. You are much more likely to find yourself worrying about your score when you are looking down, below the level of the horizon. This is where your eyes move when you want to think deep, internal thoughts, which are usually negative. Brooding introspection over mistakes and missed opportunities will almost certainly be the result.

Look up!

Contrast this with raising your chin and taking in the scene around you. This makes you think externally, a far more relaxing place for your mind to be. When Walter Hagen made his famous speech about not forgetting to smell the flowers along the way, this is very much what he was talking about. Raise your head and you will raise your game as well.

During the round, danger crops up when your mind wanders back or forward. Thinking about the future normally brings nervousness while dwelling on the past can bring anger or frustration. Tony Robins, who has worked with Tiger Woods and Andre Agassi, once said, 'Unsuccessful people create mental images of impending failure.' You must keep your thoughts in the present, but that is easier said than done, so here are some simple techniques.

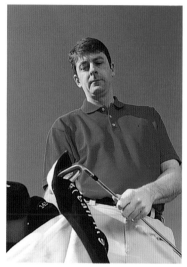

Driving

Before you step up to drive, clean the soles of your shoes. It makes you aware of the teeing ground and the ground conditions. You turn your mind with conscious attention to the now. Your thoughts hone in on the shot to come.

Fairway

Before playing a shot off the fairway, clean your clubface. This draws your attention to the club you have picked and the yardage for the shot to play. Cleaning the face of the club is a good way of showing yourself that you attach importance to the next shot.

Focus on the present

You can't change what's happened, and worrying about what may happen will increase the chances of your fears coming true. Concentrate on the task in hand and shut out everything else.

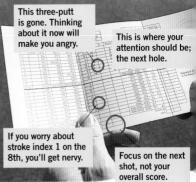

This three-putt is gone. Thinking about it now will make you angry.

This is where your attention should be; the next hole.

If you worry about stroke index 1 on the 8th, you'll get nervy.

Focus on the next shot, not your overall score.

Green

Line up the ball logo. This doesn't just help you hit the ball on-line; it also forces your mind to focus on the line. Once you have your mind on that, it will stop drifting forward to what it means to your score if you miss.

5: ACT UP

When you feel yourself getting a little jumpy, don't be afraid to try a little role-playing. Spend a few moments imagining how a cool, controlled pro would play your next shot and try to play it as they would. There's no better role model for this than Bernhard Langer.

AS USED BY...
JOHNNY MILLER

When American Johnny Miller won an amazing comeback victory in the 1994 AT&T Pro-am, aged 46, he admitted to being petrified over his final putt. Later, he explained how he had holed it. 'Johnny Miller could not hole that putt. I asked myself who could, and came up with my son Michael ... a fantastically cool putter.'

Beat set-up tension by shifting your focus

Each year as the competition season gets under way, golfers up and down the country wrestle once again with trying to play good golf when it matters. Tension is the competition golfer's worst enemy. But many golfers are unaware that they bring tension on themselves purely by the way they look at the ball! In fact there is a right and a wrong way for a golfer to do this simple thing. The wrong way leads

to worry and tension, and makes you over-aware of mechanics; the right way relaxes your muscles, keeps you calm and gives you a far better awareness of your target and what you are trying to achieve with the shot. Read on to discover how you should and shouldn't look at the ball. Shifting your focus may take a little getting used to, but once you do so, you will feel the anxiety evaporate.

Learn peripheral vision: try the machinegun drill

Line up six balls. Hit them one by one, without stopping. Swing with your normal swing speed. You will find yourself flowing through the routine without focusing on each ball. You will be hitting them in peripheral, relaxed vision.

AS USED BY... PELE

The Brazilian soccer star used to say that when he was playing football he saw the entire scene. He also had the feeling everyone around him was standing still while he was running with the ball.

HOW TO LOOK WITH RELAXED VISION

Tension is the competition golfer's worst enemy, often brought on purely by the way they look at the ball. The perfect illustration of tense vision is staring at a computer screen. Your eyes are focused sharply on one small area, which takes your attention. This is known as fovial vision. Now imagine you are on holiday, looking at a beautiful view. Your eyes are not focused on anything; you are absorbing the full scene. Your mind is relaxed and able to take in smells, sounds and feelings. This is known as peripheral vision.

TENSE VISION

RELAXED VISION

Tense

Most golfers get transfixed by the ball, staring at it as if they are trying to turn it into stone. They look at the ball with fovial, tense vision. Not only does this make it hard to relax – it also makes it hard to shift your attention to your target, or a particular swing move that you are trying to make.

You will also find yourself hitting at the ball, which means a short, stabby swing rather than a fluent followthrough. In effect, focusing on the ball will prevent you seeing the bigger picture.

Relaxed

Instead, you should look at the ball with peripheral vision, aware that the ball is there without needing to focus on it. You will find peripheral vision stops self-talk and quietens your mind. It also makes it much easier to form an awareness of where your target is and to put your swing thoughts into action. When you are in peripheral-vision mode, you will find it much easier to swing through the ball to your target. Your whole game will show an improvement.

Quick tip

There's an adage that you should let the ball get in the way of a good swing. It's a good concept. If you're getting ball-bound, work on making a smooth, well-balanced swing through the ball.

Know and use your character

Golf has the power to change your nature. I often see people behave in one way off the course and in the completely opposite way once the round begins. Loudmouths turn into mice, impulsive people become cautious and laid-back people become tense.

This change is rarely good for your game. You will shoot your best scores when you play with your normal nature, because in that frame of mind you know how to deal with the game's various highs and lows and will generally be more relaxed on the golf course. Whether you are an introvert or an extrovert it is vital that you stay true to your nature. Only then will you find yourself in a proper state of mind to play your best golf.

Introvert or extrovert?

Introverts like to deal with things quietly and internally, while extroverts prefer to share their actions and thoughts with the world. Which are you? Imagine you have just arrived at a party. An extrovert will want to head for the biggest group in the room and get involved in the conversation. An introvert will approach a small group, or someone standing on their own.

1: REACTION TO A BAD SHOT

Introvert

Dilute your anger by distracting your mind. Focus on something away from the shot – a bird flying by or a golfer on the next fairway. You'll feel just as much displeasure with your bad shot as an extrovert, but that doesn't mean you have to rant and rave. If you show emotion when it's not your nature, you will upset your balance.

Extrovert

Go ahead, show you are cheesed off with the shot. Okay, we don't need clubs thrown or rude words hollered at the top of your voice, but don't let anyone stop you from having a chunter or making some irritated action with the club. As an extrovert you must let your anger out in order to move on. Don't bottle it up.

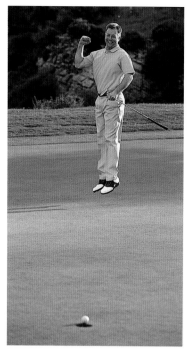

Extrovert

If you hit a good shot then, again, let your character out. Keep it within the bounds of etiquette, but punch the air, jump about, give a roar of delight. Some people seem to think it isn't seemly to make a song and dance out of a good shot; extroverts are simply best off not playing with them. You need to get that excitement out of your system. If you feel you have to coop it up, it will only come out later and louder!

Introvert

A small fist-pump or giving yourself a mental round of applause is all you need to register your pleasure. You deal with emotions internally, so jumping around will feel forced and unnatural to you. Former tennis champion Bjorn Borg described hitting a winner past McEnroe or Connors as feeling similar to getting high on the inside. The fact that he didn't show his emotions made them no less powerful.

Extrovert

Ideally you will play with other extroverts and have a darned good natter as you walk down the fairway. You will be walking for three hours or more during a round of golf and inevitably you'll spend some of that time alone. But it's important to keep expressing yourself and your emotions. You will become tense and worried if you bottle them up.

Introvert

You are happy with your own company and will be comfortable walking down the fairway alone. Do not concentrate on your game, however, while you do this; take in your surroundings instead. Walking on your own can be regarded as unfriendly and maybe you won't want to do this for 18 holes. But be sure to give yourself plenty of time alone.

Thinker or doer?

Thinkers like to weigh things up and take all factors into account before making decisions. Doers act more on instinct and impulse. Neither is better for golf – both types of person can play equally well – but it's important you keep true to your character on the course. Which are you? You buy a new computer and get it home. Thinkers like to read the instructions carefully and make sure the whole system is set up perfectly before turning it on. Doers just want to rip it out of the packing, turn it on and get started.

1: BEFORE THE ROUND

Thinker

You are going to want to spend some time hitting balls first, getting to know how your swing feels, getting used to the weather conditions and building up feel. By the time you reach the first tee you want to feel you are prepared for the round ahead. Stick with the routine that feels comfortable and don't let yourself be rushed.

Quick tip

Thinkers: don't be pushed
into rushing; give yourself the
time you need to prepare fully
for your round.
Doers: don't force yourself
into an artificial pre-round
routine. If it suits you,
keep things short.

Doer

You might hit a couple of putts and give your limbs a stretch but you want to get on with things; you will pretty much head directly to the first tee. Do not feel this means you are under-prepared – doers often get into trouble by spending too much time thinking about the round beforehand. You don't need to; your instinctive attitude is best suited to thinking on the hop.

Quick tip

Thinkers: if you're in doubt about a shot you may think too long about what might go wrong and fluff it.
Doers: if you're a confident type, trust your instincts and go for that risky shot.

Thinker

The more you look at a chancy shot, the harder it becomes. Your careful, methodical approach is ill-suited to taking chances; you will feel uncomfortable as you play the shot, which is usually enough to make any attempt unsuccessful. If you are a thinker, taking the safe option is likely to be the right one.

Doer

An instinctive player has the best chance of pulling off a risky shot because he can approach it with confidence. As a rule doers can take on a tricky snick through the trees because they don't spend time doubting themselves or considering other options.

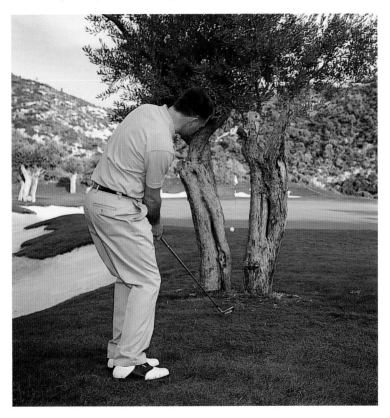

AS USED BY... **MIKE WEIR**

The 2003 Masters champ is a great thinker. On the 15th at Augusta he took all the risk out of his second shot by laying up short of the pond. The Canadian then pitched and putted for birdie and went on to win in a play-off.

Thinker

Your information-gathering nature comes to the fore here. You will be checking for wind direction, yardage, hazards, a flat part of the tee, that you have clean spikes, you name it. It is all done to put you in the best possible frame of mind to hit a successful shot, and the more info you have, the more confident you will feel.

Doer

You will put your instinctive character to its best use by hitting the ball before you have a chance to second-guess yourself. Take a look at the hole, grab a club and hit the shot. You will feel at your most positive when you allow your instinct to take over.

Stay in the present

In a four-hour round of golf there will be at least three hours when you are not actively involved in hitting a golf ball. In these moments your mind can focus on the past, future or present. In golf, the past tends to mean regret or anger while the future usually means worry and apprehension. So train your mind to stay in the present. You can only ever do anything about the next shot, so approaching it with your mind firmly on the job gives you every chance of success. The best way to anchor your thoughts in the here and now is through your senses of hearing, sight and feel. I'll show you how.

1: USE YOUR EARS

Latching on to the sounds around you will help keep you in the present moment.

◀ The Velcro rip

Before you play each shot, rip the Velcro on your glove slowly and then reseal it. Use this sound as an auditory cue for the next shot. It also narrows your focus. After just a few rips you'll find the noise starts to draw your thoughts from past and future to fix firmly on the present.

▼ Pick three sounds

As you walk up to your ball, let your ears pick out three sounds. It could be a greenkeeper's mower, a plane flying overhead, or even a bird singing. These sounds affix you to now, not to the past hole or the next hole. If you feel your mind drifting, tune into these sounds.

2: USE YOUR EYES

When you focus on sights around you, you draw your mind instantly to the present, freeing it from regrets or anxieties.

Pick three sights

As with the three sounds, let your eyes pick three sights on the hole you are playing – perhaps an unusual tree, a fairway marker or a water hazard. Aim to make what you pick out singular to the hole you are on – again, this anchors you firmly in the present moment and immerses you in the hole you are playing. It also gives you a mental break.

Focus on the present by picking out key features on each hole.

1 Let an unusual shape such as a fairway trap grab your attention.

2 Look at the height and the colour of the flagstick or fairway marker pole.

3 Examine the trees bordering the fairway. Aim to pick a type unique to the hole.

Quick tip

Those moments when you're not hitting a ball are as important as when you play a shot. Use them to sharpen your focus on the present rather than brooding on mistakes or possible problems to come.

Be a sharpshooter

When you look at your target before you hit the shot, make sure you really look at it. Take in the scene, so that when you look at the ball your mind's eye has a crystal-clear picture of where you are trying to hit it.

Keep focused

If your mind is wandering when you look at your target, your mind's eye can form only a blurry picture of it at best. What chance have you got of hitting your target when you can't even properly picture it?

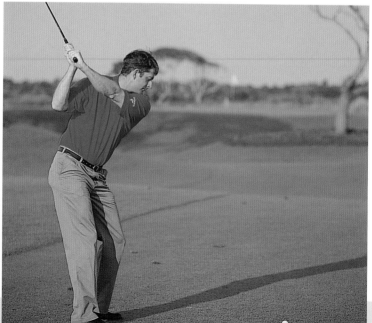

See the 'ghost ball'

When you hit a putt, you will find an image of the ball remains at its original position for a split second after you have hit it. Make a point of seeing this ghost ball after each putt. It is easy to get distracted by the success or failure of the putt, but this drill stops your mind rushing forward to see whether or not you have holed it. You will putt far more consistently as a result.

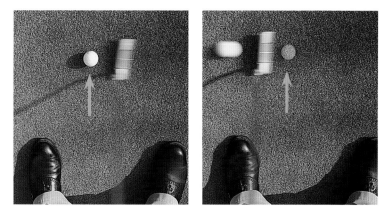

Go dotty

Draw a red dot on your glove, up around the knuckles. Before each shot, focus on the red dot. Forcing yourself to do this before each shot encourages your mind to snap straight to the shot in hand.

Quick tip

Focusing on the ghost ball after impact also keeps your head steady. It's tempting to look up quickly to see if the ball is on-line, but any early head movement can throw your putter off-line.

Let your feet and hands stop your mind racing forwards or back.

Walk the putt

On long putts, make a point of walking from the ball to the hole. Not only will this help you get a sense of the distance and borrows involved; it will also lock your mind into the specifics of this particular putt.

AS USED BY... **BERNHARD LANGER**

Former Ryder Cup captain Langer is the perfect example. Watch how he paces the putt out and looks at it from all angles. When you see how focused he is over each putt, you realize he couldn't possibly be thinking about the future or the past.

Foot feel

When you walk down the fairway, focus on the ground under your feet. Feel the springiness of the grass and the contours of the ground. Making yourself aware of where you are walking is another great way of anchoring yourself in the present moment.

Touch your head

No doubt at some stage during the round you will catch yourself thinking of a putt you missed a few holes ago, or a tricky drive to come. At this point, just touch your temple lightly as if pressing a button. As you do this, lift your head up and take in your surroundings.

Use routine to hold your putting nerve

Whether they are aware of it or not, many golfers feel uncomfortable from the moment they set foot on the green. We know that putting makes our score – a good putt can make up for a pack of hacks while a bad one can undo a lot of good work – so the heat is cranked right up. The trouble is that your rhythm, your feel, even your ability to see the line, evaporate as tension and anxiety increase. Your way out of this catch-22 is through routine. Repeating a set of actions breeds familiarity and confidence, so I want you to learn and stick to a routine every time you reach the putting surface. Follow this five-point plan for putting composure and you will feel far more chilled out on the greens. You'll hole more putts, too.

START CONCENTRATING

Use the fringe

As you approach the green, consciously look at the fringe as you step over it. This is your signal to collect your wits and start concentrating – you are entering the arena. I want you to become disciplined about when and how you turn your concentration on and off. It's amazing how many golfers, even Tour pros, go through the motions of lining up or hitting a shot before they have turned their concentration on.

Quick tip

When you walk the length of the putt, pay special attention to the slopes around the cup. Your ball will meet these when it is rolling at its slowest, and so will be more influenced by them.

Take two breaths

Walk the length of the putt. As you do so, take two deep breaths from your stomach. Deep breathing calms your mind, and this counteracts any early feelings of anxiety you may get from the difficulty of the putt – perhaps its length or a big break. Long, slow breaths also help slow you down. Okay, we don't want slow play, but tension tends to make you rush. You need to take your time at this stage.

Work out the line

Study the slopes and the speed of the green to build yourself a crystal-clear 'action-track' image of the ball rolling along the line and into the cup. Work from the hole back to the ball if you feel this helps. Never leave this stage until you can see a pin-sharp vision of the ball rolling all the way to the hole. This is something you may recognize – a picture of your putting line which starts out distinct but becomes blurry as the ball rolls towards the hole. Just stay relaxed and allow a complete image to form in your mind.

Trust your instincts

If you feel a practice stroke doesn't do anything for you, don't feel you have to make one. Step up to the ball, take your stance and hit it. This can also be useful if your head tends to fill up with mechanical thoughts while you are making your practice stroke. Keep things moving and your instincts will be able to play a more central role.

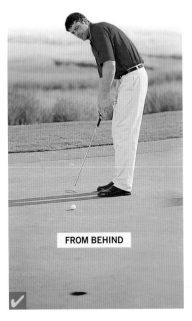

FROM BEHIND
✔

TO THE SIDE
✘

Practise from behind

Make your practice strokes from behind the ball-to-hole line, not to the side of it. This helps you make a realistic practice stroke right down the line of the putt to come. It also allows you to swivel your head from ball to hole as you will for the actual putt.

It confuses me why the preferred practice stroke is from the side of the ball. The line from this imaginary ball to the hole is different from that of the putt to come; you must adjust your aim and way you swivel your head when you move to the ball itself.

NOW RELAX

Pick up the ball

Just as looking at the fringe was your sign to start concentrating, picking up the ball is your sign to stop. Turning your mind off doesn't just preserve your precious reserves of concentration – it also stops you brooding about anything that didn't go to plan on the last hole or even earlier in the round.

You can be lucky

A book called *The Luck Factor* describes a test in which a bank note was left lying on a pavement. The testers asked five people who felt they were generally lucky to walk down the road, past the money. Each one of them spotted the tenner and picked it up. They then asked five 'unlucky' people to walk down the same stretch of road. Not one of them noticed the tenner. The test proves your attitude to luck becomes a self-fulfilling prophecy; people who think they are unlucky usually attract bad luck. Similarly, a golfer who would call himself lucky tends to have good breaks. And as good luck is far better for your scorecard than bad, it's about time you started thinking of yourself as a lucky player. Here are some effective ways to help to make fate start smiling on you.

CHECK YOUR ATTITUDE TO...

...FIRST TEE, LAST GREEN

LUCK TACTIC

Do not be afraid to label your golf equipment lucky. A 'lucky' headcover on your 3-wood can give you a boost when it comes to using that club for an important tee shot. Using a 'lucky' marker can help you feel you are about to hole a crucial putt.

Lucky? Too right!

You shake hands with your opponent on the first tee. He wishes you good luck. 'Thanks,' you reply. At this stage you are happy to have all the luck in the world – kicks off trees, bounces away from ponds, the odd kind ricochet off an out-of-bounds post. Anything the gods of golf give you will be gratefully received.

Compare this with your attitude on the 18th green, when you shake hands again. You've won one-up, and your opponent says, 'You were lucky there.' This time your tendency is to be indignant – how dare he say that? It was your good play that won it. You refute being lucky; your attitude has come full circle from the first tee. To build belief in yourself as a lucky golfer, accept the comment. Not only will this irritate your opponent, it will reinforce your confidence.

Believe

Being lucky really comes into its own when you are looking for your ball in the rough or the trees. Just like with the £10 note in the test, an 'unlucky' person is less likely to find his ball than a 'lucky' person.

An unlucky person will spend his time looking saying to himself, 'Chances are I won't find it, this always happens to me.' This narrows his focus and brings on that very eventuality.

Expect

A lucky person will walk into the bushes expecting to find the ball. And because of this he will be more open and receptive to spotting it.

It's not unusual

During a round you will hit a poor shot but come up with a good lie. Walk up to your ball like you expected it to wind up there. You are a lucky golfer, this is normal for you. And if someone calls out 'Jammy git', just smile and agree with them.

LUCK TACTIC

Most golfers come off the course thinking they have been very unlucky. Such an attitude has repercussions for their next round, invariably attracting the bad fortune they moan about. Do not fall into this trap. Review every round and pick three moments when fate smiled on you. Mark what happened on your scorecard (not the official one you have to hand in!). This will help you see yourself as a fortunate player and breed good luck in return.

On the 4th green you have a 30ft putt for birdie. You smack the ball way too hard, but it hits the hole, jumps into the air, then dives into the hole.

A golfer who feels he is lucky will behave as if he expected it. His body language will say 'I'm a lucky golfer, these sort of things happen to me.' Make this your reaction.

A golfer who considers himself unlucky will react by covering his face with his hands or looking skyward. He is effectively saying to himself, 'But I'm unlucky, this is not supposed to happen to me, it must have been a one-off.'

Control your emotions

As a breed, Tour pros get a bad press. They are often called bland, characterless, boring, undemonstrative. I would look at it another way. To play golf at a high standard you need to have complete mastery over yourself and your actions; the need for self-control is one of the things that makes golf such a great challenge. You simply will not get the best out of your game if you are seething with rage one minute and bubbling with joy the next. Here are some easy ways to control your emotions on the course. They won't turn you into a robot, but they will help you maintain your equilibrium – a vital commodity over 18 holes and four hours of golf.

1: PLEASURE
HOW TO TAG IT...

When you hit a good shot, it's important you give your body every chance to remember how you did it. Introducing a movement as you watch the ball fly true is a great way to anchor the shot – it makes the shot special, one that stands out. This helps your muscles recall it. Here are two methods the pros use:

Tap the ground
Just give the turf a gentle kick with your toe cap as the ball soars off. The tap says to your memory, 'We'll have that one, store it.'

AS USED BY...
TIGER WOODS

You may have noticed Tiger give the ground a little kick with his back foot when he nails a drive down the fairway. He is telling his muscles, 'Remember that one – it worked.'

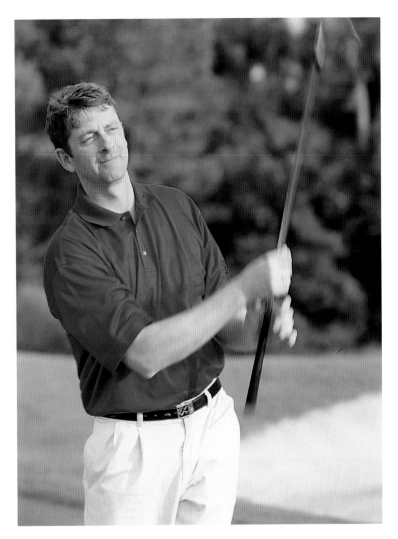

Spin the club in your hands

As you watch the ball fly to the pin, spin the grip with your fingers.

HOW TO LET IT GO...

Frustration creeps up on you. A series of disappointments over the course of
the round can make you short-tempered and affect your decision-making. It's
important that you keep releasing frustration through the round – otherwise it'll
store up and bite you before you know it.

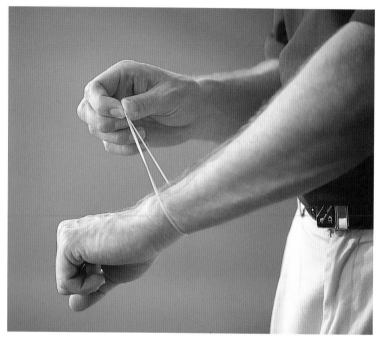

Ping an elastic band

Wear an elastic band on your wrist – not too tight, we don't want your hands turning blue.
When you feel frustration growing, stretch the band and let it snap back on to your wrist.
Let the release of the band represent to you a release from any pressure and frustration
you are feeling.

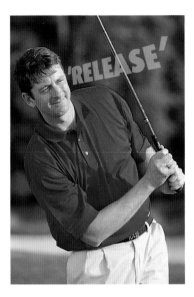

Say 'release'

Just saying the word can help you flush away your frustration. Choose your own phrase when you feel irritation nibbling at you – it could be the word 'easy' or 'let it go'.

Press 'delete'

Imagine your head has a delete button, just like your PC keyboard. Pressing the button is your cue to rid your head of all frustrations that have stored up.

HOW TO LET IT GO...

As far as good scoring is concerned, anger is as useful to you as the sockets of your irons. Anger means loss of control, and no one ever played good golf when they weren't in charge of what they were doing. Relax and let go.

Quick tip

Learn to control your anger before it controls you. You'll play your best when you can relax and enjoy, taking each shot as it comes.

Hold your finish for seven seconds

Most bursts of anger happen immediately after the shot is hit. Make it a rule to hold your followthrough position until you count to seven. This stops you flinging clubs around or burying them in the turf. It also forces you to keep your eye on the ball, vital when it's headed for the rough.

Do not even begin to assess the shot until you have counted to seven. By this time you will be in a more resourceful state, one where you find yourself able to learn from what went wrong rather than rant at your miscue.

Controlled release

There are times when bottling up your anger actually does you more harm than good. Having a little go at yourself can help release some of the anger you feel, so set yourself up an 'anger zone' in which you are permitted to let off some steam. Pick a pitchmark or divot ten yards or so in front of you. This spot represents the end of your 'anger zone'. Tell yourself that once you are past that line you will leave your fury behind.

HOW TO BREATHE EASY...

Fear makes you tense and tight, maximizing your chances of hitting the bad shot you're afraid of. Here are some tips to help you relax.

Take deep breaths

There's nothing new in breathing deeply to calm yourself, but it really works and is easy to forget under pressure. Fear makes you want to take lots of small, shallow breaths from your chest; inhaling deeply from your stomach sends more oxygen around your body, slows you down and calms your nerves.

Squeeze the sponge

Imagine your golf grip is a sponge that you are trying to squeeze every drop of water out of. Once you've got all the water out, your hands will naturally relax and you are ready to play the shot. It can help to say 'Ssshhh...' to yourself while you relax.

Be a copycat

Imagine you are trying to hit a 7-iron shot like Tiger Woods. How would your swing change from what it is normally? Perhaps it would become crisper, more compact. Maybe you would feel more 'punchy' through the ball. Perhaps your legs would feel stronger, more stable; or your swing might feel smoother. One thing's for sure – it would feel better. Okay, you may never swing it quite like your heroes, but mimicking their attitudes and techniques can improve yours dramatically. I want you to experiment with becoming a golfing chameleon – adopting different personas for different situations.

CRUCIAL PUTTS

COPY JOSE MARIA OLAZABAL

When sizing up a crucial putt, see yourself making a confident stroke and holing out.

It doesn't matter how critical the putt, Ollie always gives you the impression he's going to hole it. His mannerisms are positive, deliberate, unhurried. There is never any indecision. He looks calm, confident, up to the job. When you face an important putt, set about it like Ollie would. Make your body language purposeful, like his. Make your practice strokes count. Take your time. Too many amateurs who don't enjoy short putts rush them. Tell yourself you are up to it and enjoy the challenge. Above all, make a crisp, positive stroke.

A typical Ollie pose – relaxed, positive, purposeful. Build these attributes into your stroke.

COPY SEVE BALLESTEROS

Seve's positive body language helps him meet the challenge and see escape routes.

Picture how the best in the world would tackle your recovery.

Watching Seve get out of trouble during his heyday was magical. His shoulders never dropped because of his predicament – no, he invariably saw it as a personal challenge to make the best recovery possible. His enthusiasm for the test translated into energetic body language as he prowled around looking for openings and opportunities. Build a similar energy into your recovery strategy. Positive and energetic body language will help you see opportunities and give you the belief to pull the shot off.

COPY ERNIE ELS

Ernie's unhurried trap technique makes him your perfect bunker role model.

When you picture Ernie playing from sand you see a slow, almost casual action as the club splashes into the sand behind the ball. The whole thing is fluent and comfortable, the very opposite of the tense, frantic body language many amateurs adopt in sand.

If you find yourself getting jumpy in traps, play sand shots like Ernie. Keep your swing long and unhurried. Experiment with how fluently you can swing while still splashing the ball out. Simply making a calm pass at the ball can help you feel calm, which helps you avoid an ugly and ineffectual thrash.

COPY TIGER WOODS

Tiger's iron play is superb. He makes a short, compact swing. Although he hits the ball aggressively he is always in control. He stays perfectly balanced through the swing and commits completely to the shot, holding his followthrough until the ball lands.

When you must hit the green, call on your 'Tiger' swing. Rehearse it with three practice swings. Keep your action short, punchy and manageable. Make sure your weight stays balanced. Perhaps take an extra club to be sure your controlled swing will send the ball back to the pin. Watch the ball through the air until it lands – even if it is missing the green.

Use this image to help you make a compact, controlled and balanced backswing turn.

COPY BERNHARD LANGER

Langer is probably the best in the world at dealing with disaster. However terrible his shot, his expression hardly changes. Because he remains calm, he is able to make the right decisions at this vital time and minimize the damage.

When you mess up, turn into Bernhard. Make your face stony, expressionless. Slow your actions down. Make a commitment to being as unruffled as the German, keeping your mind clear of anger and frustration. Instead, adopt Langer's deliberate and careful policy of selecting your best way out of trouble. It will pay dividends.

Mind myths

If there's all kinds of bad advice out there concerning golfing technique the same is true in terms of attitude, and once again it can do more harm than good. We can end up assuming that certain feelings and actions on course are more or less inevitable, when in fact they're the last thing we need. This final section highlights just a few of the common errors we can fall into. Learn its lessons and you'll approach your next round in an altogether different state of mind, ready not only to play your best but, above all, to enjoy your game as you should.

'COMPETITION HAS TO BE SERIOUS'

Below is a familiar image from any monthly medal or competition. You trudge off the green alone, absorbed with your score, and without saying a word to your playing partner. There seems to be some unwritten rule in golf that as soon as you have a scorecard in your hands you must look as if you are about to top yourself.

Lighten up!

Think how much better you'd feel if you walked off the green having a laugh.
It means you can really enjoy a good hole and helps put a bad one behind you.
It is possible to smile and take your round seriously. You play your best golf while having fun.

MIND MYTH 2

'A ROUND OF GOLF MEANS FOUR HOURS OF CONCENTRATION'

Okay, golf is a hard game, but there is nothing to be gained by burying yourself deep in thought the moment you leave the first tee. You'll be drained by the time you reach the 6th green. You'll also drown yourself in swing thoughts and doubts. That won't help.

Ration your concentration

You only have so much concentration in you, so you must learn to focus when you need to and relax when you don't. Think of your concentration as a bottle of water. Every time you concentrate, you dribble water out of your bottle. While you are relaxing, the bottle is upright. Your job is to make your water last the whole round.

Take in the surroundings...

... concentrate on the shot.

Take a break

Next time you walk up to your ball on the green, make yourself relax. Forget about the shot to come and drink in your beautiful surroundings.

The time to concentrate comes when you reach your ball. You will find yourself much more able to focus because you have given your brain a breather.

'WHAT YOU FEEL IS WHAT YOU DO'

If I was to ask you how long your backswing is, I'm sure you could tell me. No doubt you have a picture in your mind. But that image is wrong. Your backswing ends after you think it does because of the momentum you have built up. This can cause an overswing and loss of control.

BRAKE HERE... ...TO STOP HERE!

Think of it as car braking distances

The Highway Code tells us that if you start braking at 60mph it takes you 240 feet to stop. It's the same with your backswing. You must aim to stop it before you really want it to end. Even though your backswing feels short, you will in fact end up making a controlled and full turn.

'IGNORE HAZARDS'

Take a look at this situation. I have trees and sand both sides of the pin.
The usual advice you'll hear is to put the hazards out of your mind and focus
on your target. But your mind doesn't work that way. Tell yourself to ignore
something and you end up thinking about it.

Use hazards to frame your target

Instead, why not use them to define your target? Think of those bunkers and trees as guides, framing your route to the pin like lights on a runway guiding the pilot in the dark. This gives you a much clearer mental image of your target when you are stood over the ball.

Adrian Fryer

Growing up within a short pitch from Worsley Golf Club in Greater Manchester, Adrian was soon captivated by the game, despite neither of his parents being golfers. In 1984 and aged just 22 he was appointed full-time club professional at Chorley Golf Club in Lancashire where, despite his considerable promise as a player, his fascination with golf technique and uncanny ability as an instructor led him to focus on his role as a teacher. An avid researcher into the latest training methods, he swiftly developed distinctive coaching ideas of his own, communicating these through local and subsequently regional newspapers.

Fryer's reputation continued to spread as he moved first to Warrington Golf Club and later to the Drivetime driving range where he helped set up the innovative Drivetime Golf School and the PGA teaching conference. Through intensive video analysis he explored the mechanics of swing technique in a way few had even begun to, his ideas opening up new horizons in golf tuition. His big break came in 1999 when contributions to *Golf World* magazine led to an invitation to write for its sister magazine *Today's Golfer*. Since then Adrian's career has blossomed, his regular 'Team TG', 'Golf Doctors' and 'Learn to Play Golf' features having found a ready audience the world over.

Adrian has also designed and patented various golfing aids, chief among them being the 'Swingmatic' – a revolutionary training tool for the short game. Renowned today as one of Europe's top golf coaches, he has not only assisted numerous world-class golfers but has also helped thousands of ordinary players to improve their game beyond recognition.

Karl Morris

Dr Karl Morris has earned widespread recognition as one of Europe's foremost sports psychologists, helping a range of clients from the world of business as well as sport to optimize their levels of performance. His remarkable ability to translate in-depth knowledge of neuro-linguistic programming (NLP) into practical and effective advice has led to a host of top players enlisting his services, including Darren Clarke, Paul McGinley, Ian Woosnam, Charl Schwartzel, Paul Eales, Simon Dyson, Graeme McDowell, Alison Nicholas and Trish Johnson.

Currently working as golf psychologist with the English Ladies Golf Association, he is also a qualified PGA professional, having conducted seminars across the world as well as serving as a consultant to the PGA of Great Britain and Europe, for which he has written the national mental-skills training programme Ideal Performance Project. His books include *Golf Mind* (with Ian Woosnam), *Golf – The Mind Factor* (with Darren Clarke) and *Masterstroke*. He has also authored the CD series *Train your Golf Brain* and writes regularly for the *Today's Golfer* magazine.

Sports psychologists like Karl have opened up a whole new dimension in terms of what's involved in achieving success. He has ably demonstrated that a positive mental attitude and ability to handle pressure is as important as having the correct technique.

Index